D0775236

INTO THE LOOKING-GLASS WOOD

INTO THE LOOKING-GLASS WOOD

BY

ALBERTO MANGUEL

ALFRED A. KNOPF CANADA

PUBLISHED BY ALFRED A. KNOPF CANADA

 Published in Canada by Alfred A. Knopf Canada, Toronto. Distributed by Random House of Canada Limited, Toronto.

Canadian Cataloguing in Publication Data
Manguel, Alberto, 1948-
Into the looking-glass wood : essays on words and the world
ISBN 0-676-97135-0

1. Literature and society. I. Title.

PN45.M345 1998 809 C98931238-0

Printed and bound in the United States of America
10 9 8 7 6 5 4 3 2 1

To Lenny Fagin,
best of friends, who was there
in the very beginning.

"But what happens when you come to the beginning again?" Alice ventured to ask.

Alice's Adventures in Wonderland, Chapter VII

TABLE OF CONTENTS

"They drew all manner of things—
everything that begins with an M—"

"Why with an M?" said Alice.

"Why not?" said the March Hare.

Alice's Adventures in Wonderland, Chapter VII

TABLE OF CONTENTS

I

FOREWORD

"You ought to return thanks in a neat speech," the Red Queen said, frowning at Alice as she spoke.

Through the Looking-Glass, Chapter IX

With Thanks

FOR ME, WORDS ON A PAGE give the world coherence. When the inhabitants of Macondo were afflicted with an amnesia-like sickness which came to them one day during their hundred years of solitude, they realized that their knowledge of the world was quickly disappearing and that they might forget what a cow was, what a tree was, what a house was. The antidote, they discovered, lay in words. To remember what their world meant to them, they wrote out labels and hung them from beasts and objects: "This is a tree," "This is a house," "This is a cow, and from it you get milk, which mixed with coffee gives you *café con leche*." Words tell us what we, as a society, believe the world to be.

"Believe to be": therein lies the challenge. Pairing words with experience and experience with words, we, readers, sift through stories that echo or prepare us for an experience, or tell us of experiences that will never be ours (as we know all too well) except on the burning page. Accordingly, what we believe a book to be reshapes itself with every reading. Over the years, my experience, my tastes, my prejudices have changed: as the days go by, my memory keeps reshelving, cataloguing, discarding the volumes in my library; my words and my world—except for a few constant landmarks—are never one and the same. Heraclitus's *bon mot* about time applies equally well to my reading: "You never dip into the same book twice."

What remains invariable is the pleasure of reading, of holding a book in my hands and suddenly feeling that peculiar sense of wonder, recognition, chill or warmth that for no discernible reason a certain string of words sometimes evokes. Reviewing books, translating books, editing anthologies are activities that have provided me some justification for this guilty pleasure (as if pleasure required justification!) and sometimes even allowed me to make a living. "It is a fine world and I wish I knew how to make £200 a year in it," wrote the poet Edward Thomas to his friend Gordon Bottomley. Reviewing, translating and editing have sometimes allowed me to make those £200.

Henry James coined the phrase "the figure in the carpet" for the recurrent theme that runs through a writer's work like a secret signature. In many of the pieces I have written (as reviews or memoirs or introductions) I think I can see that elusive figure: it has something to do with how this craft I love so much, the craft of reading, relates to the place in which I do it, to Thomas's "fine world." I believe there is an ethic of reading, a responsibility in how we read, a commitment that is both political and private in the act of turning the pages and following the lines. And I believe that sometimes, beyond the author's intentions and beyond the reader's hopes, a book can make us better and wiser.

Craig Stephenson, who for the past years has been the first reader of everything I've written, suggested the structure, order and selection for this book. He curbed my inclination to keep occasional pieces to which I was attached for sentimental reasons, and reminded me of others that I had forgotten, and spent far more time reflecting on the appropriateness of each piece than I myself, in my impatience, would have done. For this, and for more things than he would ever be willing to acknowledge, my loving thanks.

Many of the pieces here collected have appeared, over the years, in various shapes and guises, in a number of publications whose hospitality I wish to acknowledge.

"Jonah and the Whale" and "The Age of Revenge" were conceived as talks given at the Banff Centre for the Arts, where I was head of the Maclean-Hunter Arts Journalism Programme from 1991 to 1995; the latter piece appeared, slightly modified, in the *Svenska Dagbladet*, Stockholm. "Meanwhile, in Another Part of the Forest" and "The Gates of Paradise" were the introductions to two anthologies, one of gay stories (edited with Craig Stephenson) and one of erotic short fiction. An earlier draft of "On Being Jewish" was published in the *Times Literary Supplement* of London, as were "The Death of Che Guevara," "The Blind Photographer" and a shorter version of "St. Augustine's Computer"; the latter was delivered as the *TLS* lecture in 1997. "Imagination to Power!" appeared as the afterword to my translation of Julio Cortázar's *Unreasonable Hours*, and then was expanded to introduce a volume of his selected stories, published under the title *Bestiary*. Earlier versions of "Browsing in the Rag-and-Bone Shop" (under the title "Designer Porn"), "Waiting for an Echo" (under the title "Hard Words") and "The Secret Sharer" appeared in *Saturday Night* magazine, Toronto. "Reading White for Black" (under the title "A Blind Eye and a Deaf Ear") appeared both in *Brick* and in *Index on Censorship*. The latter also published an early version of "God's Spies" as an answer to Vargas

Llosa's call for amnesty in Argentina. "Dragon Eggs and Phoenix Feathers" and "The Muse in the Museum" appeared in *Art Monthly*, Melbourne. "In Memoriam" was published by *Heat* magazine, Sydney. "The Irresolutions of Cynthia Ozick" combines several reviews of her work published in the New York *Village Voice* and the Toronto *Globe and Mail*. "Taking Chesterton at His Word" was written as an introduction to my selection of Chesterton essays for the Italian publishing company Adelphi and first published in the *Frankfurter Rundschau*. A section of "Borges in Love" appeared in *The Australian's Review of Books*.

In spite of my views on editing declared in "The Secret Sharer," most of these pieces have benefited greatly from the generous and intelligent readings of a number of devoted magazine and newspaper editors, too many to name but all of whom I humbly thank. If the craft of editing required a *raison d'être*, it would be, in my case, my friendship with Louise Dennys, whose passion for good writing, good stories and what Stevenson called the "ultimate decency of things" I have learned to treasure over the past many years. Any errors, solecisms, unshapeliness and blots are entirely my own.

And, as usual, my thanks to the unflagging team at Westwood Creative Artists, *semper fidelis*.

ALBERTO MANGUEL, Calgary, fall 1998

II

WHO AM I?

"I *am* real!" said Alice, and began to cry.

"You won't make yourself a bit realer by crying," Tweedledee remarked: "there's nothing to cry about."

"If I wasn't real," Alice said—half-laughing through her tears, it all seemed so ridiculous—"I shouldn't be able to cry."

"I hope you don't suppose those are real tears?" Tweedledum interrupted in a tone of great contempt.

Through the Looking-Glass, Chapter IV

A Reader in the Looking-Glass Wood

"Would you tell me, please, which way I ought to go from here?"

"That depends a good deal on where you want to get to," said the Cat.

Alice's Adventures in Wonderland, Chapter VI

Man's innate casuistry!
To change things by changing their names!

KARL MARX
quoted in *The Origins of the Family*,
by Friedrich Engels

WHEN I WAS EIGHT OR NINE, in a house that no longer stands, someone gave me a copy of *Alice's Adventures in Wonderland & Through the Looking-Glass*. Like so many other readers, I have always felt that the edition in which I read a book for the first time remains, for the rest of my life, the original one. Mine, thank the stars, was enriched by John Tenniel's illustrations and was printed on thick creamy paper that reeked mysteriously of burnt wood.

There was much I didn't understand in my first reading of *Alice*—but that didn't seem to matter. I learned at a very early age that, unless you are reading for some purpose other than pleasure (as we all sometimes must for our sins), you can safely skim over difficult quagmires, cut your way through tangled jungles, skip the solemn and boring lowlands, and simply let yourself be carried by the vigorous stream of the tale. Alice, who couldn't see the use of a book "without pictures or conversations," would surely agree.

As far as I can remember, my first impression of the adventures was that of a physical journey on which I myself became poor Alice's companion. The fall down the rabbit-hole and the crossing through the looking-glass were merely starting points, as trivial and as wonderful as boarding a bus. But the journey! When I was eight or nine, my disbelief was not so much suspended as yet unborn, and fiction felt at times more real than everyday fact. It was not that I thought that a place such as Wonderland actually existed, but I knew that it was made of the same stuff as my house and my street and the red bricks that were my school.

A book becomes a different book every time we read it. That first childhood *Alice* was a journey, like the *Odyssey* or *Pinocchio*, and I've always felt myself a better Alice than an Odysseus or a wooden puppet. Then came the adolescent *Alice*, and I knew exactly what she had to put up with when the March Hare offered her wine when there was no wine at the table, or when the Caterpillar wanted her to tell him exactly *who* she was and *what* she meant by that. Tweedledee and Tweedledum's warning, that Alice was nothing but the Red King's dream, haunted my sleep, and my waking hours were tortured with exams in which Red Queen teachers asked me questions like "What's French for fiddle-de-dee?" Later, in my twenties, I found the Knave of Hearts' trial collected in André Breton's *Anthologie de l'humour noir*, and it became obvious that Alice was a sister of the surrealists; after a conversation with the Cuban writer Severo Sarduy in Paris, I was startled to discover that Humpty Dumpty owed much to the structuralist doctrines of *Change* and *Tel Quel*. And later still, when I made my home in Canada, how could I fail to recognize that the White Knight ("But I was thinking of a plan/ To dye one's whiskers green,/ And always use so large a fan/ That they could not be seen") had found a job as one of the numerous bureaucrats that scurry through the corridors of every public building in my country?

In all the years during which I've read and reread *Alice*, I've come across many other different and interesting readings of her books, but I can't say that any of these have become, in any deep sense, my own. The readings of others influence, of course, my personal reading, offer new points of view or colour certain passages, but mostly they are like the comments of the Gnat who keeps naggingly whispering in Alice's ear, "You might make a joke on that." I refuse; I'm a jealous reader and will not allow others a *jus primae noctis* with the books that I read. The intimate sense of kinship established so many years ago with my first Alice hasn't weakened; every time I reread her, the bonds strengthen in very private and unexpected ways. I know bits of her by heart. My children (my eldest daughter is, of course, called Alice) tell me to shut up when I burst, yet again, into the mournful strains of "The Walrus and the Carpenter." And for almost every new experience, I find a premonitory or nostalgic echo in her pages, telling me once again, "This is what lies ahead of you" or "You have been here before."

One adventure among many describes for me not any particular experience I've had or may one day have, but rather seems to address something vaguer and vaster, an experience or (if the term is not too grand) a philosophy of life. It takes place at the end of chapter three of *Through the Looking-Glass*. After passing through her reflection and making her way across the chessboard country that lies behind it, Alice reaches a dark wood where (she has been told) things have no names. "Well, at any rate it's a great comfort," she says bravely, "after being so hot, to get into the—into the—into *what*?" Astonished at not being able to think of the word, Alice tries to remember. "'I mean to get under the—under the—under *this*, you know!' putting her hand on the trunk of a tree. 'What *does* it call itself, I wonder? I do believe it's got no name—why, to be sure it hasn't.'" Trying to recall the word for the place she is in, accustomed to putting into words her experience of reality, Alice suddenly discovers that nothing actually has a name: that until she herself can name something, that thing will remain nameless, present but silent, intangible as a ghost. Must she remember these forgotten names? Or must she make them up, brand-new? Hers is an ancient conundrum.

After creating Adam "out of the dust of the ground" and placing him in a garden east of Eden (as the second chapter of Genesis tells us), God went on to create every beast of the field and every fowl of the air, and brought them to Adam to see what he would call them; and whatever Adam called every living creature, "that was the name thereof." For centuries, scholars have puzzled over this curious exchange. Was Adam in a place (like the Looking-Glass Wood) where everything was nameless, and was he supposed to invent names for the things and creatures he saw? Or did the beasts and the fowl that God created indeed have names, which Adam was meant to know, and which he was to pronounce like a child seeing a dog or the moon for the very first time?

And what do we mean by a "name"? The question, or a form of the question, is asked in *Through the Looking-Glass*. A few chapters after crossing the nameless wood, Alice meets the doleful figure of the White Knight who, in the authoritarian manner of adults, tells her that he will sing a song to "comfort" her. "The name of the song," says the Knight, "is called '*Haddocks' Eyes*.'"

> "Oh, that's the name of the song, is it?" Alice said, trying to feel interested.
>
> "No, you don't understand," the Knight said, looking a little vexed. "That's what the name is *called*. The name really is '*The Aged Aged Man*.'"
>
> "Then I ought to have said 'That's what the *song* is called'?" Alice corrected herself.
>
> "No, you oughtn't: that's quite another thing! The song is called '*Ways and Means*': but that's only what it's *called*, you know!"
>
> "Well, what *is* the song then?" said Alice, who was by this time completely bewildered.
>
> "I was coming to that," the Knight said. "The song really is '*A-sitting On a Gate*': and the tune's my own invention."

As it turns out, the tune *isn't* his own invention (as Alice points out) and neither are the Knight's careful distinctions between what a name is called, the name itself, what the thing it names is called and the thing itself; these distinctions are as old as the first commentators of Genesis. The world into which Adam was inducted was innocent of Adam; it was also innocent of Adam's words. Everything Adam saw, everything he felt, as everything he fancied or feared was to be made present to him (as, eventually, to every one of us) through layers of names, names with which language tries to clothe the nakedness of experience. It is not by chance that, once Adam and Eve lost their innocence, they were obliged to wear skins "so that," says a Talmudic commentator, "they might learn who they were through the shape that enveloped them." Words, the names of things, give experience its shape.

The task of naming belongs to every reader. Others who do not read must name their experience as best they can, constructing verbal sources, as it were, by imagining their own books. In our book-centred societies, the craft of reading signals our entrance into the ways of the tribe with its particular codes and demands, allowing us to share the common source of recorded words; but it would be a mistake to think of reading as a merely receptive activity. On the contrary: Mallarmé proposed that every reader's duty was "to purify the sense of the words of the tribe." To do this, readers must make books theirs. In endless libraries, like thieves in the night, readers pilfer names, vast and marvellous creations as simple as Adam and as far-fetched as Rumpelstiltskin. A writer will tell us, as Proust does, that the volumes of Bergotte's library keep watch over the dead artists throughout the night, in pairs like guardian angels; but it is the reader of Proust who, alone one night in the darkened bedroom, sees those angels' wings betraying their presence, outlined in the sweep of passing headlights. Bunyan describes Christian running from his house with his fingers in his ears, so as not to hear the pleas of his wife and children; Homer describes Ulysses, bound to the mast, trying in vain to shut out the sirens' song; the reader of Bunyan and Homer names with these words the deafness of our contemporary, the amiable Prufrock. Edna St. Vincent Millay calls herself "domestic as a plate" and it is the reader who renames the daily kitchen china, the companion of his meals, with a newly acquired meaning.

As every child knows, the world of experience (like Alice's wood) is nameless, and we wander through it in a state of bewilderment, our head full of mumblings of learning and intuition. The books we read assist us in naming a stone or a tree, a moment of joy or despair, the breathing of a loved one or the kettle-whistle of a bird, by shining a light on an object, a feeling, a recognition, and saying to us that this here is our heart after too long a sacrifice, that there is the cautionary sentinel of Eden, that what we heard was the voice that sang near the Convent of the Sacred Heart. These illuminations sometimes help; the order of experiencing and naming doesn't much matter. The experience may come first and, many years later, the reader will find the name to call it in the pages of *King Lear*. Or it may come at the end, and a glimmer of memory will throw up a page we had thought forgotten of a battered copy of *Treasure Island*. There are names made up by writers that a reader refuses to use, because they seem wrong-headed, or trite or even too great for ordinary understanding, and are therefore dismissed or forgotten, or kept for some crowning epiphany that (the reader hopes) will one day require them. But sometimes, they help the reader name the unnamable. "You want him to know what cannot be spoken, and to make the perfect reply, in the same language," says Tom Stoppard in *The Invention of Love*. Sometimes a reader can find on a page that perfect reply.

The danger, as Alice and her White Knight knew, is that we sometimes confuse a name and what we call a name, a thing and what we call a thing. The graceful phantoms on a page, with which we so easily tag the world, are not the world. There may be no names to describe the torture of another human being, the birth of one's child. After creating the angels of Proust or the nightingale of Keats, the writer can say to the reader "into your hands I commend my spirit," and leave it at that. But how is a reader to be guided by these entrusted spirits to find his way in the ineffable reality of the wood?

Systematic reading is of little help. Following an official book list (of classics, of literary history, of censored or recommended reading, of library catalogues) may, by chance, throw up a useful name, as long as we bear in mind the motives behind the lists. The best guides, I believe, are the reader's whims—trust in pleasure and faith in haphazardness—which sometimes lead us into a makeshift state of grace, allowing us to spin gold out of flax.

Gold out of flax: in the summer of 1935 the poet Osip Mandelstam was granted by Stalin, supposedly as a favour, identity papers valid for three months, accompanied by a residence permit. According to his wife, Nadezhda Mandelstam, this little document made their lives much easier. It happened that a friend of the Mandelstams, the actor and essayist Vladimir Yakhontov, chanced to come through their city. In Moscow he and Mandelstam had amused themselves by reading from ration books, in an effort to name paradise lost. Now the two men did the same thing with their identity papers. The scene is described in *Hope Against Hope*:

> It must be said that the effect was even more depressing. In the ration book they read off the coupons solo and in chorus: "Milk, milk, milk ... cheese, meat ..." When Yakhontov read from the identity papers, he managed to put ominous and menacing inflections in his voice: "Basis on which issued ... issued ... by whom issued ...special entries ... permit to reside, permit to reside, permit to reside ..."

All true readings are subversive, against the grain, as Alice, a sane reader, discovered in the Looking-Glass world of mad name-givers. A Canadian prime minister tears up the railway and calls the act "progress"; a Swiss businessman traffics in loot and calls it "commerce"; an Argentinian president shelters murderers and calls it "amnesty." Against such misnomers a reader can open the pages of his books. In such cases, reading helps us maintain coherence in the chaos, not to eliminate it; not to enclose experience within verbal structures but to allow it to progress on its own vertiginous way; not to trust the glittering surface of words but to burrow into the darkness.

The poor mythology of our time seems afraid to go beneath the surface. We distrust profundity, we make fun of dilatory reflection. Images of horror flick across our screens, big or small, but we don't want them slowed down by commentary: we want to watch Gloucester's eyes plucked out but not have to sit through the rest of *Lear*. One night, some time ago, I was watching television in a hotel room, zapping from channel to channel. Perhaps by chance, every image that held the screen for a few seconds showed someone being killed or beaten, a face contorted in anguish, a car or a building exploding. Suddenly I realized that one of the scenes I had flicked past did not belong to a drama series but to a newscast on Bosnia. Among the other images which cumulatively diluted the horror of violence, I had watched, unmoved, a real person being hit by a real bullet.

George Steiner suggested that the Holocaust translated the horrors of our imagined hells into a reality of charred flesh and bone; it may be that this translation marked the beginning of our inability to imagine another person's pain. In the Middle Ages, for instance, the horrible torments of martyrs depicted in countless paintings were never viewed simply as images of horror: they were illumined by the theology (however dogmatic, however catechistic) that bred and defined them, and their representation were meant to help the viewer reflect on the world's ongoing suffering. Not every viewer would necessarily see beyond the mere prurience of the scene, but the possibility for deeper reflection was always present. After all, an image or a text can only *offer* the choice of reading further or more profoundly; this choice the reader or viewer can reject since, in themselves, text and image are nothing but dabs on paper, stains on wood or canvas.

The images I watched that night were, I believe, nothing but surface; like pornographic texts (political slogans, Bret Easton Ellis's *American Psycho*, advertising pap), they offered nothing but what the senses could apprehend immediately, all at once, fleetingly, without space or time for reflection.

Alice's Looking-Glass Wood is not made of such images: it has depth, it requires thought, even if (for the time of its passage) it offers no vocabulary to name its proper elements. True experience and true art (however uncomfortable the adjective has become) have this in common: they are always greater than our comprehension, even than our capabilities of comprehension. Their outer limit is always a little past our reach, as the Argentinian poet Alejandra Pizarnik once described:

> And if the soul were to ask, How much further?
> You must answer: on the other side of the river,
> Not this one, the one just beyond.

To come even that far, I've had many and marvellous guides. Some overwhelming, such as Borges; others more intimate, such as Cortázar or Cynthia Ozick; many vastly entertaining, such as Chesterton or Stevenson; a few illuminating more than

I could hope to see, such as Richard Outram. Their writing keeps changing in the library of my memory where circumstances of all sorts—age and impatience, different skies and different voices, new and old readings—keep shifting the volumes, crossing out passages, adding notes in the margins, switching jackets, inventing titles. I'm reminded of the moralist Joseph Joubert whose reading habits were described by Chateaubriand: "When he read, he would tear out of his books the pages he didn't like, assembling in this way a personal library made up of gutted volumes bound under baggy covers." The furtive activity of such anarchic librarians expands my limited library almost to infinity: I can now reread a book as if I were reading one I had never read before. In Bush, his house in Concord, the seventy-year-old Ralph Waldo Emerson began suffering from what was probably Alzheimer's disease. According to his biographer, Carlos Baker:

> Bush became a palace of forgetting ... [But] reading, he said, was still an "unbroken pleasure." More and more the study at Bush became his retreat. He clung to the comforting routine of solitude, reading in his study till noon and returning again in the afternoon until it was time for his walk. Gradually he lost his recollection of his own writings, and was delighted at rediscovering his own essays: "Why, these things are really very good," he told his daughter.

Something like Emerson's rediscovery happens now when I take down *The Man Who Was Thursday* or *Dr. Jekyll and Mr. Hyde*, and meet them like Adam greeting his first giraffe.

Is this all? Sometimes it seems enough. In the midst of uncertainty and many kinds of fear, threatened by loss, change and the welling of pain within and without for which one can offer no comfort, readers know that at least there are, here and there, a few safe places, as real as paper and as bracing as ink, to grant us roof and board in our passage through the dark and nameless wood.

On Being Jewish

"Well, now that we *have* seen each other," said the Unicorn, "if you'll believe in me, I'll believe in you. Is that a bargain?"

Through the Looking-Glass, Chapter VII

ONE AFTERNOON, when I was seven, on the bus back from the Buenos Aires English high school that I had started to attend, a boy whose name I never knew called out at me from the back seat, "Hey, Jew, so your father likes money?" I remember being so bewildered by the question that I didn't know what to answer. I didn't think my father was particularly fond of money, but there was an implied insult in the boy's tone that I couldn't understand. Above all, I was surprised at being called "Jew." My grandmother went to the synagogue, but my parents were not religious, and I had never thought of myself in terms of a word I believed was reserved for the old people of my grandmother's generation. But since the epithets applied to us imply a definition, in that moment (though I didn't know it then) I was forced into a choice: to accept this vast, difficult identity, or to deny it. The French philosopher Alain Finkielkraut, in an effective mingling of sociological essay and autobiography, *The Imaginary Jew*, tells of a similar moment and acknowledges the universality of such an experience, but his subject is not the inheritance of hatred. "I myself," writes Finkielkraut, "would like to address and meditate upon the opposite case: the case of a child, an adolescent who is not only proud but happy to be Jewish and who came to question, bit by bit, if there were not some bad faith in living jubilantly as an exception and an exile." These individuals of assumed identity, the inheritors of a suffering to which they have not been personally subjected, Finkielkraut, with a flair for the *mot juste*, calls "imaginary" or "armchair Jews."

I am struck by how useful this notion is to address a question that troubles me: how does the perception of who I am affect my perception of the world around me? How important is it for Alice to know who she is (the Victorian child that the world perceives her to be) when wandering through the Looking-Glass Wood? Apparently, very important, since this knowledge determines her relationship to the other creatures she encounters. For instance, having forgotten who she is, Alice can become friends with a fawn who has forgotten it is a fawn.

> So they walked on together through the wood, Alice with her arms clasped lovingly round the soft neck of the Fawn, till they came out into another open field, and here the Fawn gave a sudden bound into the air, and shook itself free from Alice's arm. "I'm a Fawn!" it cried out in a voice of delight. "And, dear me! you're a human child!" A sudden look of alarm came into its beautiful brown eyes, and in another moment it had darted away at full speed.

Around this notion of constructed identity, Finkielkraut has assiduously elaborated a sequence of questions about what it means to be Jewish (or, I would add, to be Alice or a fawn) and, since every definition is a limitation, he has refused to give these questions definitive answers. Central to Finkielkraut's interrogation is the seemingly trite statement that the Jews *exist*, that whatever their identity may be, individually or as a group, they have a presence that not even the Nazi machinery was able to erase. This existence is not easily borne, let alone categorized. "Listen, Doctor," wrote Heinrich Heine, "don't even talk to me about Judaism, I wouldn't wish it on my worst enemy. Slurs and shame: that's all that comes of it. It's not a religion, it's a misfortune." The cry "Why me?" uttered by every persecuted Jew, the imaginary Jew picks up with a sigh of ennui. Using himself as an example, Finkielkraut confesses that on the one hand he broadcasts his wish to be a Jew, while on the other hand he de-Judaizes himself, transforming himself into the Other and becoming a messenger of his gentile companions: in this I vividly recognize myself. When his parents refer to the Holocaust, he responds with Vietnam; when they mention anti-Semitism, he points out that there are no Jewish garbage collectors in France. "Why me?" has become "Why am I not someone else?"

In this Looking-Glass Wood, the imaginary Jew has lost all sense of belonging; for him there is no possible Jewish "we." The conventions of prejudice understand this "we" to mean a secret society of infamous plots and world domination; his response has been to deny solidarity. "There is no 'we,'" he declares, "for Judaism is a private affair"—even though today it once again widely recognizes itself as a community. But why, Finkielkraut asks pointedly, must collective expression "always remain the exclusive province of politics? Why would anything that is not 'I' necessarily be a question of power or of state?" Why can the Jew not be "I" without either going into hiding or making claims to belonging to the slaughtered millions of the past?

These are dangerous waters. Perhaps it is not the necessity to remember the ancestral persecutions that is called into question, but the illusion of heroism it so often entails. Those who profess contempt for their fellows living "in the forgetfulness of history," forget in turn that their own precarious identity rests on "the phantasm of history." On the vaporous webbing of such a past, a past that blesses all Jews with a multitudinous family far in time and vast in space, younger Jews sometimes feel they are nothing but spectators. Watching my grandmother light the Shabbath candles, say the ritual prayers as her hands drew opposing circles over the startled light, I felt no connection to the dark, ancient places of wood and winter mist and ancient languages from which she had come. She was my grandmother, but her existence started and ended in my present; she rarely spoke of her ancestors or of the place where she was born, so that in my mythology her brief, piecemeal stories had far less bearing on my life than the landscapes of Grimm and Alice.

If Judaism has a central injunction, Finkielkraut argues, it should be not "a matter of identity, but of memory: not to mimic persecution or make theater of the Holocaust, but to honor its victims," to keep the Holocaust from becoming banal, so that the Jews are not condemned to a double death: by murder and by oblivion. Even here, my connection to those horrors was vicarious: to my knowledge, we lost no immediate family to the Nazis; both my mother's and my father's parents had immigrated long before World War I to one of the colonies set up by Baron Hirsch in the north of Argentina, where gauchos with names like Izaak and Abraham called out to their cattle in Yiddish. I didn't learn about the Holocaust until well into my adolescence, and then only by reading André Schwarz-Bart and Anne Frank. Was this horror then part of my history too, mine beyond the call of a shared humanity? Did the epithet hurled at me insultingly on that remote school bus grant me citizenship in that ancient, beleaguered, questioning, stubborn, wise people? Was I—am I—part of Them? Am I a Jew? Who am I?

Alice, a human child, and the fawn, one of the hunted, echo this last question, and like me are tempted to answer it not with words born from what they know themselves to be, but with words coined by those who stand outside and point. Every group that is the object of prejudice has this to say: we are the language in which we are spoken, we are the images in which we are recognized, we are the history we are condemned to remember because we have been barred from an active role in the present. But we are also the language in which we question these assumptions, the images with which we invalidate the stereotypes. And we are also the time in which we are living, a time from which we can't be absent. We have an existence of our own, and we are no longer willing to remain imaginary.

Meanwhile, in Another Part of the Forest

The Seventh Square is all forest—however, one of the Knights will show you the way.

Through the Looking-Glass, Chapter II

IN THE DAYS WHEN I was an avid reader of comic books, the line that thrilled me most, because it promised to reveal something that had been taking place beyond the more obvious bits of the plot, was "Meanwhile, in another part of the forest ..."—usually inked in capital letters in the top left-hand corner of the box. To me (who, like any devoted reader, wished for an infinite story) this line promised something close to that infinity: the possibility of knowing what had happened on that other fork of the road, the one not taken, the one less in evidence, the mysterious and equally important path that led to another part of the adventurous forest.

I. Mapping the forest

Damn braces. Bless relaxes.

WILLIAM BLAKE

In the middle of the third century B.C., the Cyrene poet Callimachus undertook the task of cataloguing the half-million volumes housed in the famous Library of Alexandria. The task was prodigious, not only because of the number of books to be inspected, dusted, and shelved, but because it entailed the conception of a literary order that was supposed somehow to reflect the vaster order of the universe. In attributing a certain book to a certain shelf—Homer to "Poetry" or Herodotus to "History," for example—Callimachus had first to determine that all writing could be divided into a specific number of categories or, as he called them, *pinakes*, "tables"; and then he had to decide to which category each of the thousands of unlabelled books belonged. Callimachus divided the colossal library into eight "tables," which were to contain every possible fact, conjecture, thought, imagination ever scrawled on a sheet of papyrus; future librarians would multiply this modest number to infinity. Jorge Luis Borges recalled that in the numeric system of the Institut Bibliographique in Brussels, number 231 corresponded to God.

No reader who has ever derived pleasure from a book has much confidence in these cataloguing methods. Subject indexes, literary genres, schools of thought and style, literatures classified by nationality or race, chronological compendiums and thematic anthologies suggest to the reader merely one of a multitude of points of view, none comprehensive, none even grazing the breadth and depth of a mysterious piece of writing. Books refuse to sit quietly on shelves: *Gulliver's Travels* jumps from "Chronicles" to "Social Satire" to "Children's Literature," and will not be faithful to any of these labels. Our reading, much like our sexuality, is multifaceted and fluid. "I am large," wrote Walt Whitman, "I contain multitudes."

The notion of "gay literature" is guilty on three counts: first, because it implies a narrow literary category based on the sexuality of either its authors or its characters; second, because it implies a narrow sexual category that has somehow found its definition in a literary form; third, because it implies a narrow political category that defends a restricted set of human rights for a specific sexual group. And yet the notion of "gay literature," albeit recent, doubtlessly exists in the public mind. Certain bookstores have "gay literature" shelves, certain publishers publish "gay literature" series, and there are magazines and papers that regularly bring out stories and poems under the rubric of "gay literature."

What then is this "gay literature"?

At the risk of committing a tautology, what is in general understood by "gay literature" is literature concerned with gay subjects. This can swing from obscure hints about "the love that dare not speak its name," in Lord Alfred Douglas's self-silencing phrase, apparent in some nineteenth-century writing, to explicit chronicles of gay life in our time by authors who may or may not be gay. Sometimes books dealing with non-gay subjects by gay writers (E. M. Forster's *A Passage to India*, Edward Albee's *Who's Afraid of Virginia Woolf*, for instance) are put on the same "gay literature" shelf as books with an explicitly gay content—Marguerite Yourcenar's *Alexis* or Manuel Puig's *Kiss of the Spider Woman*—as if the critic, editor, or bookseller were deliberately attempting to catalogue the person, not the person's work. Certain writers refuse to have their work labelled "gay" (Patrick Gale, Timothy Findley) and refer to it as "books by a writer who happens to be gay." As usual with this kind of labelling, the exceptions to any proposed definition make the process finally useless, so that every time the label is applied it must be redefined.

Claude J. Summers, in his collection of essays *Gay Fictions*, defines his subject as "the fictional representation of male homosexuals by gay male and lesbian writers." This leaves out a fair number of works by non-gay writers, which are thus excluded simply by reason of their authors' sexuality. A writer's sexual preferences probably colour the text, but a reader does not require careful study of the *National Enquirer* to be able to read literature. Being told that D. H. Lawrence was attracted to older women may or may not inform the enjoyment of *Lady Chatterley's Lover*, but is in no way essential for reading that too-famous novel. A study of Melville's life might shed light on homoerotic elements in *Moby-Dick*, but is such a study essential in order to discover those same elements? And is a short story by William Faulkner on a gay subject readable only if we have proof of his experience in this field? Doesn't the word "fiction" imply the creation of an imagined rather than a physically experienced world? And if knowledge of the author's inclinations is essential to the understanding of a text, wouldn't reading anonymous literature (and so much erotic literature is anonymous) be ultimately impossible?

II. Paths through the forest

> The fairy way of writing which depends only upon
> the force of imagination.
>
> JOHN DRYDEN, *King Arthur*

Borges said that "every writer creates his own precursors." The same is true for genres or types. Edgar Allan Poe invented the detective story, and in doing so allowed us to include in the definition tales as old as the Bible. The label "gay literature" is a recent creation, probably no older than the founding of the gay magazine *Christopher Street* in 1975, but it now includes much earlier work. An anthology of English-language gay poetry would feature many names from the traditional canon, from

Shakespeare to Lord Byron; examples of English-language gay fiction are not as venerably old, perhaps because poetry lends itself more readily to an ambiguous reading and (as is the case in many spurious explanations of Shakespeare's homoerotic sonnets) to a bigoted interpretation, while prose can be less easily subverted for the sake of social decorum. Thomas Hardy suggested that a writer could "get away with things in verse that would have a hundred Mrs. Grundys on your back if said in prose."

A chronological list of gay fiction in English might begin with obscure novels such as Bayard Taylor's *Joseph and His Friend* (1871) or Theodore Winthrop's *Cecil Dreme* (1876), or with better-known works such as Oscar Wilde's "The Portrait of Mr. W. H." (a short story written *circa* 1890); it might continue with Henry James's almost too subtle depiction of a gay infatuation, "The Pupil" (1891), E. M. Forster's posthumously published *Maurice* (finished in 1914), D. H. Lawrence's "The Prussian Officer" (also 1914), and Ronald Firbank's *Concerning the Eccentricities of Cardinal Pirelli* (1926), up to Gore Vidal's *The City and the Pillar*, one of the earliest mainstream fictional accounts of gay life, published in 1948—the year that also saw the publication of two other gay classics: Truman Capote's *Other Voices, Other Rooms* and Tennessee Williams's collection *One Arm and Other Stories*. Similar lists could be made in the literature of other languages.

By 1950, two main trends in English-language gay literature had been established: one apologetically addressing a "straight" audience, trying to justify and atone for the fact of being gay; the other unabashedly celebrating another, equally vital sexuality, and speaking mainly to an enlightened reader. *The City and the Pillar*, which follows both trends to some degree, is the first novel to make use of an important device (suggested perhaps by André Gide's *Si le grain ne meurt* of 1926) evident in almost all the gay fiction that follows it: the autobiographical voice. Edmund White, himself the author of one of the most influential gay autobiographical fictions in North America, *A Boy's Own Story* (1982), has remarked that "since no one is brought up to be gay, the moment he recognizes the difference he must account for it." Non-gays learn about their sexual mores (mostly from conservative, sexist sources) in hundreds of different places: home, school, workplace, television, film, print. Gays are, by and large, deprived of any such geography. They grow up feeling invisible, and must go through the apprenticeship of adolescence almost invariably alone. Gay fiction—especially autobiographical gay fiction—therefore serves as a guide that both reflects and allows comparison with the reader's own experience.

Much of this factual prose is illuminating and encouraging (something much needed in the age of AIDS), and allows the reader to admit the fact of being gay as part of everyday life. Camille Paglia has commented that most gays, unlike other minority groups, do not reproduce themselves, and therefore, like artists everywhere, "their only continuity is through culture, which they have been instrumental in building." Authors such as Christopher Isherwood (*A Single Man*), David Leavitt (*The Lost Language of Cranes*), and Armistead Maupin (in his soap-opera saga *Tales of the City*) make this "continuity through culture" explicit: they place their gay characters in the midst of a multifaceted society, so that their reality is not "other" but "another," part of a historical cultural whole, with no reigning central entity determining what is normal according to his own image.

Because of the instructional use to which gay literature can be put, gay stories that bow to prejudice, implicitly accepting the patriarchal verdict about the wages of sin, commit literary terrorism and deserve to be housed on the same shelf as moralistic Victorian fables. A number of good writers fall into this category: Dennis Cooper, for instance, whose fiction depicts necro-homoerotic longings and explores the aesthetics of sickness and decay, with death as the inevitable end; and at times the timorous Gide, who believed that homosexuality was "an error of biology," and whose heroes are so terribly ridden by Catholic angst.

Because it needs to instruct, because it needs to bear witness, because it needs to affirm the right to exist of a group that the power-holding majority of society wishes to ignore or eliminate, most gay literature has been staunchly realistic. Lagging behind the rights demanded and partly achieved by other oppressed groups, gay men are depicted in a literature that is still largely at an informative or documentary stage. Women's literature can produce fantasies, such as Margaret Atwood's *The Handmaid's Tale* or Jeanette Winterson's *The Passion*; black literature can invent ghost stories, such as Toni Morrison's *Beloved*; with one or two superb exceptions (Wilde's *The Portrait of Dorian Gray* and Genet's *Our Lady of the Flowers* come immediately to mind) gay literature has no fantastic stories, no imaginary worlds. Instead, its strength lies in the subversive possibilities of its language.

Appropriating everyday language, undermining the bureaucratic use of common words, using the guerrilla tactics of the surrealists to fill the commonplace with a sense of danger—these are the things gay literature, like any literature of the oppressed, can do best. Jean Genet, the French poet, playwright and novelist who died in 1985, created, better than any other gay writer in any language, a literary voice to explore the gay experience. Genet understood that no concession should be made to the oppressor. In a hypocritical society that condemns gay sexuality but condones the exploitation of women, arrests pickpockets but rewards robber barons, hangs murderers but decorates torturers, Genet became a male prostitute and a thief, and then proceeded to describe the outcast's vision of our world as a sensual hallucination. This vision was so unsettling that when Jean Cocteau showed Paul Valéry the manuscript of Genet's *Our Lady of the Flowers*, Valéry's response was "Burn it." In English, Oscar Wilde, Joe Orton, William Burroughs—all forced or voluntary outsiders of society—set social language against its overlords.

Perhaps the literature of all segregated groups goes through similar stages: apologetic, self-descriptive and instructive, political and testimonial, iconoclastic and outrageous. If that is the case, then the next stage, which I think can be recognized in certain novels by Alan Gurganus or Alan Hollinghurst, introduces characters who *happen to be gay* but whose circumstances are defined well beyond their sexuality, which is once again seen as part of a complex and omnivorous world.

III. Marking the trees

> Years hence, perhaps, may dawn an age,
> More fortunate, alas! than we,
> Which without hardness will be sage,
> And gay without frivolity.
>
> MATTHEW ARNOLD,
> "Stanzas from the Grande Chartreuse"

Naked except for a fur-trimmed gauze negligée and waddling about in bare feet, Cary Grant announced to an enquiring May

Robson that he was thus attired because he had gone "gay." With this pronouncement in the 1939 film *Bringing Up Baby*, the word "gay," meaning "male homosexual," publicly entered the English language of North America.

It was not an auspicious beginning. Cary Grant's usage reflected a stereotype: that being "gay" somehow involves dressing up in women's clothing, wishing to be the other sex, and consequently becoming an involuntary parody of a woman. No doubt some gay men dress up in drag, but all transvestites are not homosexual, and all homosexuals are certainly not transvestites. Society, for the majority of Cary Grant's audience, appeared to be an immutable reality in which men and women fulfilled certain specific roles, dressed in specific ways, and reacted in a specific manner, and the questioning of the necessity of these roles and styles was seen as deviant—and therefore wrong. Today, some of these perceptions have changed but the changes have been mostly superficial. Beneath the apparently tolerant manners of Cary Grant's new audiences, the same traditional standards continue to rule and the same old discomfort continues to be felt.

The historical origins of this meaning of the word "gay" are somewhat dubious. *Gai savoir* meant "poetry" in thirteenth-century Provençal, and as some troubadour poems were explicitly homosexual, it is possible that the word came to designate this particular aspect of their repertoire. Other inquisitive etymologists have traced its origins to Old English, where one of the meanings of the word *gal* was "lustful," as in modern German *geil*. Whatever the sources, by the early twentieth century "gay" was commonly used in English homosexual subculture as a password or code. Nowadays, "gay" or *gai* is the usual term for "male homosexual" in French, Dutch, Danish, Japanese, Swedish, and Catalan.

"Gay" is reserved for male homosexuality. Female homosexuality—lesbianism, to use the term still ignored in the 1971 edition of the *Oxford English Dictionary*—has a vocabulary and career of its own. In spite of the prejudice that views all unconventional sexualities as part of the same herd of sinners, and in spite of the common political force that results from being the object of such a prejudice, male and female homosexualities differ in their public image, their vocabularies, and their histories. Lesbianism, for instance, is empowered by its association with feminism—gay males have no such support from any equivalent male group—and lesbian acts are ignored in certain heterosexual codes of law; Britain's notorious anti-homosexual laws of the past century were designed exclusively for males, as Queen Victoria (tradition has it) refused to believe "that women did such things." In most countries, female couples are considered "respectable" while male couples are unthinkable except as an abomination, perhaps because in the heterosexual male imagination that dominates most societies, two women living together do so only because they haven't been able to acquire a man, and are either to be pitied for this shortcoming, or to be praised for undertaking, on their own, tasks that are normally a man's responsibility. Similarly, lesbian images are accepted—in fact, encouraged—in heterosexual male pornography, the fantasy being that these women are making love among themselves in expectation of the male to come. The heterosexual male code of honour is thereby preserved.

A person not complying with these pre-set codes seemingly threatens the received identity of the individuals who uphold these codes in their society. In order to dismiss the transgressor with greater ease, it is best to caricature him (as the success of such pap as *La Cage aux Folles* seems to prove), thereby creating the myth of the Good Homosexual. The Good

Homosexual, as in Harvey Fierstein's *Torchsong Trilogy*, is the man who deep down inside wants to be like his mother—have a husband, have a child, putter around the house—and is prevented from doing these things by a quirk of nature. Underlying the myth of the Good Homosexual is the conviction (upheld by the American Psychological Association until 1973) that a homosexual is a heterosexual gone wrong: that with an extra gene or so, a little more testosterone, a dash of tea and sympathy, the homosexual will be cured, become normal. And if this cannot be achieved (because in some cases the malady is too far advanced), then the best thing for the creature to do is assume the other, lesser role designed by society in its binary plan: that of an ersatz woman. I remember a psychological test set for my all-boys class by a school counsellor concerned with "particular friendships." A previous class had warned us that, if we drew a female figure, the counsellor would assume that our fantasy was to be a woman; if we drew a male figure, that we were attracted to a man. In either case we would be lectured on the terrors of deviancy. Deviants, the counsellor had told the other class, always ended up murdered by sailors on the dockside. When my turn came, I drew the figure of a monkey.

IV. The forest in history

> ... and warming his hands to the fire exclaimed,
> "Now where would we be without faggots?"
>
> SIR WALTER SCOTT, *Kenilworth*

Homosexuality is not always socially condemned. In other societies human sexuality was known to cover a larger spectrum. In ancient Greece and Rome, no moral distinction was made between homosexual and heterosexual love; in Japan, gay relationships were formally accepted among the samurai; in China, the emperor himself was known to have male lovers. Among the native people of Guatemala, gays are not seen as outsiders: "Our people," said the native leader Rigoberta Menchú, "don't differentiate between people who are homosexual and people who aren't; that only happens when we go out of our society. What's good about our way of life is that everything is considered a part of nature."

In European society, hostility against gays did not become widespread until the mid-twelfth century. "The causes of this change," wrote Yale historian James Boswell, "cannot be adequately explained, but they were probably closely related to the increase in intolerance of minority groups apparent in ecclesiastical and secular institutions throughout the thirteenth and fourteenth centuries." And yet in spite of this hostility, until the nineteenth century the homosexual was not perceived as someone distinct, someone with a personality different from that of the heterosexual, someone who could be persecuted not only for a specific act *contra natura* but merely for existing. Until then, noted Michel Foucault in his *History of Sexuality*, "the sodomite had been a temporary aberration; the homosexual was now a species."

With the invention of the species "homosexual," intolerance created its quarry. Once a prejudice is set up, it traps within its boundaries a heterogeneous group of individuals whose single common denominator is determined by the prejudice itself. The colour of one's skin, one's varying degrees of alliance to a certain faith, a certain aspect of one's sexual preferences, can and do become the obverse of an object of desire—an object of hatred. No logic governs these choices: prejudice can couple an Indonesian lawyer and a Rastafarian poet as "coloured people," and exclude a Japanese businessman as "an honorary white"; revile an Ethiopian Jew and an American Hassid, yet pay homage to Solomon and David as pillars of the Christian tradition; condemn a gay adolescent and poor Oscar Wilde, but applaud Elton John and ignore the homosexuality of Leonardo da Vinci and Alexander the Great.

The group created by prejudice comes into existence not by the choice of the individuals forming it, but by the reaction of those outside it. The infinitely varying shapes and shades of sexual desire are not the pivot of everyone's life, yet gay men find themselves defined through that single characteristic—their physical attraction to others of the same sex—notwithstanding that those who attract them run the entire gamut of the human male—tall, short, thin, fat, serious, silly, rough, dainty, intelligent, slow-witted, bearded, hairless, right-wing, left-wing, young, old—with nothing in common except a penis. Once limited and defined by this grouping, the quarry can be taunted, excluded from certain areas of society, deprived of certain rights, sometimes arrested, beaten, killed. In England, the promotion of homosexuality is illegal; in Argentina, gays are routinely blackmailed; in the U.S. and Canada their inclusion in the armed forces is contested; in Cuba they are imprisoned; in Saudi Arabia they are put to death. In Germany, homosexuals who were victimized by the Nazis are still denied restitution, on the grounds that they were persecuted for their criminal, not political, activities.

A group, a category, a name, may be formed and transformed throughout history, but direct experience of this isn't necessary for a writer to express that experience in artistic terms—to compose a poem, to write a novel. Many stories touching on a gay theme stem from writers forced to exist within the gay ghetto. But many others have been written by men and women who have not been condemned to such enclosures. As works of fiction, they are indistinguishable from one another.

V. Variations in the landscape

Variety is the soul of pleasure.

MRS. APHRA BEHN, *The Rover*, Part II

The fourth book of the *Odyssey* tells of Proteus, King of Egypt, known as "the Ancient One of the Sea," able to tell the future and to change shape at will. According to one version of the story, he was the first man, imagined by the gods as a creature of endless possibilities. Like the apparent shapes of that ancient king, our desire need not be limited. Heterosexuality and homosexuality were no doubt two of those protean forms, but they are neither exclusive nor impermeable. Like our literary tastes, our sexual affinities need only declare allegiance and define themselves under duress. In the moment of pleasure, we are as indefinable as the moment itself. Perhaps that generous sense of pleasure will ultimately prevail.

Our social organizations, however, still demand labels, require catalogues, and these unavoidably become hierarchies and class systems in which some assume power and others are excluded. Every library has its shadow: the endless shelves of books unchosen, unread, rejected, forgotten, forbidden. And yet the exclusion of *any* subject from literature, whether by design of the reader or of the writer, is an inadmissible form of censorship that degrades everyone's humanity. The groups ostracized by prejudice may be, and usually are, cut off, but not for ever. Injustice, as we should have learned by now, has a curious effect on people's voices. It lends them potency and clarity and resourcefulness and originality, which are all good things to have if one is to create a literature.

III

MEMORANDA

"The horror of that moment," the King went on,
"I shall never, *never* forget!"

"You will, though," the Queen said, "if you don't
make a memorandum of it."

Through the Looking-Glass, Chapter I

Borges in Love

A young woman in the audience: "Mr. Borges, have you ever been in love?"

Borges (unhesitatingly): "Yes."

Yale University, March 1971

ONE AFTERNOON IN 1966, in Buenos Aires, I was asked to dinner at the flat of the writer Estela Canto. A woman of about fifty, a little deaf, with wonderful, artificially red hair and large, intensely myopic eyes (she coquettishly refused to wear glasses in public), she stumbled through the small, grimy kitchen putting together a meal of tinned peas and sausages, shouting bits of Keats and Dante Gabriel Rossetti. To her, Borges had dedicated one of his finest short stories, "The Aleph," and she would let no one forget it.

Borges, however, did not apparently reciprocate the memory. At least when I mentioned her name and told him I would be seeing her, he said nothing: someone told me later that for Borges, silence was a form of courtesy. I had met Borges a year or so earlier, at Pygmalion, the Anglo-German bookstore in Buenos Aires at which I worked after school. Accompanied by his aged mother, Borges would shuffle into the bookstore and in a groping voice ask for books on Anglo-Saxon (his latest passion) which he would then bring up to touch his face as if his nose could inhale the letters he could no longer see. One afternoon, Borges asked me (as he did so many others) if I was free in the evenings and whether I would come and read to him, since his mother grew easily tired. I accepted, unaware of the privilege.

Over many nights I read him Stevenson, Kipling, entries in the *Brockhaus Encyclopaedia*, various annotated editions of Dante, while Borges would interrupt and comment, more for his own sake than for mine, providing me as it were with a private annotated edition of his classics. He tried to persuade me to join him in the study of Anglo-Saxon, but I never got further than the first three lines of "The Battle of Maldon." Sometimes he'd ask me to accompany him to the cinema and it was a strange experience for me to sit next to the blind old man, narrating the film in a casual way as if I were merely commenting on the plot and the photography. I quickly learned that Borges didn't like a straightforward account of what was taking place on the screen, and I had to invent circumlocutions, such as "He looks so menacing, the way he comes into the room," or "Panning over the city like that is very effective, don't you think?" while the *sh* around us grew angrier and louder like a menacing wind. Together we sat through *West Side Story* (which he had already attended several times and very much enjoyed), *The Collector*, and *Lord Jim*, and he'd compare them to the films he'd seen when his eyes were still serviceable: *She Done Him Wrong* (he thought Mae West far superior to either Jean Harlow or Marlene Dietrich), *Psycho* ("Literature can't touch this kind of sustained suspense") and *King Kong* ("Fay Wray contributed not only to the monkey's downfall, but also to the downfall of the film"). Afterwards, we'd walk back to his flat while Borges, who enjoyed remembering, would describe the city as it had been when he could see, telling stories of hoodlums in dusky bars on dangerous corners over which now rose, invisible to him, the glass towers of the Sheraton Hotel and the latest designer store. When I told him that a well stood now in the middle of the touristy Plaza San Telmo, in the old colonial part of town, he didn't believe me. "You wouldn't have a well in a public plaza; wells are built in private patios, inside the house, no?" I imagined a documentary (I suggested it to Ric Young, who was then making films in Canada) in which the camera would record the present and over it Borges's voice would narrate the past, taking the viewer through the streets that he and Estela Canto had walked two decades earlier. But alas, no Canadian television station could see the merit in such a journey.

By the time I met Estela, her books were no longer considered part of the Argentinian literary scene. In the wake of the so-called Latin-American "boom" that had launched Manuel Puig's generation, editors no longer wanted to publish her and her novels now sold at remainder prices in stores as dusty as her kitchen. Long ago, in the forties, she had written essays in the style of Hazlitt (whom she admired) for several of the literary periodicals of the time, from the *Anales de Buenos Aires*, which Borges edited for a while, to *Sur*. Her realistic stories which echoed (she thought) Andreiev's, had been published in the literary supplements of the newspapers *La Nación* and *La Prensa*, and her novels, which hesitated between psychology and symbolism, had been well reviewed, if not read, by the Buenos Aires intelligentsia. According to Estela, her downfall was caused by her being too clever. With her brother Patricio Canto, an excellent translator who discreetly encouraged rumours of sibling incest, she devised a plan to win a literary contest juried by Borges, the novelist Eduardo Mallea and the poet and literary host, Norah Lange. The two Cantos would write a novel with something to please everyone: a quotation from Dante for Borges, a philosophical discussion on art, literature and morals for Mallea, a verse by Norah Lange for Norah Lange. They hid behind the name of a literary lady in whose loyalty they believed, and submitted the manuscript, which was unanimously awarded the first prize. Unfortunately, artistic friendships being what they are, the literary lady betrayed them, the plot was revealed and the conspiring siblings were ostracized from every literary *salon* in Buenos Aires. Partly out of spite and partly out of a misguided fondness for Russian literature, the Cantos joined the Argentinian Communist Party (which, Ernesto Sábato once said, was indistinguishable from the Conservative Party because most of its senile members attended its meetings asleep). Communism, to Borges, who in his regretted youth had written a book of poems in praise of the Bolshevik Revolution, was anathema.

During the dinner, Estela asked me if I would like to see the manuscript of "The Aleph" (which twenty years later she would sell at Sotheby's for $27,760). I said I would. From a grease-aureoled brown folder she pulled out seventeen pages meticulously composed "in the handwriting of a dwarf" (as Borges once described his minuscule, unattached letters), with a few minor corrections and alternative versions. She pointed to the dedication inscribed on the last page. Then she reached over the table, took my hand (I was eighteen and terrified) and put it to her cheek. "Feel these bones," she ordered. "You can tell I was beautiful then."

"Then" was 1944, the year Estela met Borges at the house of Bioy Casares and Silvina Ocampo. Silvina, a fine poet and better short-story writer, was the sister of Victoria Ocampo, the rich and aristocratic founder of the magazine *Sur*. Bioy, eight years younger than Silvina, was the heir to one of the largest dairy empires in Argentina. His mother's name, Marta, became the dairy trademark La Martona; Borges and Bioy's first collaboration had been a series of ads for La Martona yoghurt.

Estela's first encounter with Borges was, from her point of view, far from a *coup de foudre*. "And yet," she added with a nostalgic smile, "neither was Beatrice much impressed with Dante."

As if to justify her reaction, Estela's description of the forty-five-year-old Borges (later published in her memoir, *Borges a contraluz*) was deliberately unappealing. "He was plump, rather tall and straight-backed, with a pale and fleshy face, remarkably small feet and a hand that, when clasped, seemed boneless, limp, as if uncomfortable when having to bear the inevitable touch. The voice was shaky, it seemed to grope for words and seek permission." I once had occasion to hear Borges use the shakiness of his voice to great effect, when a journalist asked him what he admired most in General San Martín, Argentina's national hero, who had fought against the Spanish in the wars of independence. Borges answered, very slowly, "His bronze busts … that decorate … public offices …and school … playgrounds; his name … repeated … endlessly … in military … marches; his face … on the ten-peso … bill …" There was a long pause during which the journalist sat bewildered. Just as she was about to ask for an explanation of such a curious choice, Borges continued, "… have distanced me from the true image of the hero."

After the night of her first meeting with Borges, Estela often had dinner at the Bioys', dinners at which the conversation was lively, since Silvina had the unsettling habit of springing questions on her guests, such as "How would you commit suicide, given the choice?" The food, however, was atrocious: a few boiled vegetables and milk jam for dessert. It was common knowledge that, unless one wanted to starve, one should always have something to eat before dining at the Bioys'. Once, the critic Enrique Pezzoni hungrily sneaked into the kitchen and discovered in the refrigerator, which he had been told was bare, two steaks. Furious at what he considered intolerable stinginess, he grabbed the steaks and threw them behind the stove. For weeks after, the Bioys complained about an atrocious stench.

Borges, a frugal eater, was usually in attendance at these dinners. He maintained that eating well distracted from the conversation. His favourite food was what he called "unobtrusive fare": boiled rice or pasta with butter and a sprinkling of cheese. One summer evening, as he and Estela were by chance leaving together, Borges asked if he could walk her to the subway. At the station, Borges, stuttering, suggested that they might walk a little farther. An hour later they found themselves in a café on Avenida de Mayo. Obviously, the talk turned to literature and Estela mentioned her admiration for *Candida*, and quoted a section from the end of the play. Borges was enchanted and remarked that this was the first time he'd met a woman fond of Bernard Shaw. Then, peering at Estela through his incipient blindness he paid her a compliment in English: "A Gioconda smile and the movements of a chess knight." They left as the café was closing and walked till three-thirty in the morning. The next day Borges deposited at her house, without asking to see her, a copy of Conrad's *Youth*.

Borges's courting of Estela Canto lasted a couple of years, during which, she said, "he loved me and I was fond of him." They would go for long walks or for aimless tram rides across the southern neighbourhoods of Buenos Aires. Borges was fond of trams: it was on the number 7 tram, on his way to and from his miserable job at a municipal library, that he taught himself Italian by reading a bilingual edition of Dante's *Commedia*. "I started Hell in English; by the time I had left Purgatory I was able to follow him in the original." When he wasn't with Estela, he wrote to her, incessantly, and his correspondence, which she later included in *Borges a contraluz*, is quietly moving. One undated letter, apologizing for having left town without letting her know "out of fear or courtesy, through the sad conviction that I was for you, essentially, nothing but an inconvenience or a duty," goes on to confess: "Fate takes on shapes that keep repeating themselves, there are circling patterns; now this one appears again: again I'm in Mar del Plata, longing for you."

In the summer of 1945 he told her that he wanted to write a story about a place that would be "all places in the world," and that he wanted to dedicate the story to her. Two or three days later he brought to her house a small package which, he said, contained the Aleph. Estela opened it. Inside was a small kaleidoscope which the maid's four-year-old son immediately broke.

The story of the Aleph progressed along with his infatuation with Estela. He wrote to her, on a postcard, in English:

> Thursday, about five.
>
> I am in Buenos Aires. I shall see you tonight, I shall see you tomorrow, I know we shall be happy together (happy and drifting and sometimes speechless and most gloriously silly), and already I feel the bodily pang of being separated from you, torn asunder from you, by rivers, by cities, by tufts of grass, by circumstances, by days and nights.
>
> These are, I promise, the last lines I shall allow myself in this strain; I shall abound no longer in self-pity. Dear love, I love you; I wish you all the happiness; a vast

> and complex and closewoven future of happiness lies ahead of us. I am writing like some horrible prose poet; I don't dare to reread this regrettable postcard. Estela, Estela Canto, when you read this I shall be finishing the story I promised you, the first of a long series.
>
> Yours,
> Georgie

"The story of the place that is all places" (as Borges calls it in another postcard) begins with the summer of the death of the beautiful Buenos Aires aristocrat Beatriz Viterbo, with whom Borges, the narrator, is in love. Beatriz's cousin, the pedantic and bombastic poet Carlos Argentino Daneri (it was rumoured that Borges based the character on his brother-in-law, the writer Guillermo de Torre, who faithfully subscribed to the vocabulary recommended by the Royal Spanish Academy of Letters) is composing a huge epic poem that will include everything on earth and in heaven; his source of inspiration is the Aleph, a place in which all existence has been assembled. This place, Daneri tells Borges, is under the nineteenth step down to Beatriz's basement and one must lie on the floor in a certain position in order to see it. Borges complies, and the Aleph is revealed to him. "The diameter of the Aleph would not have been more than two or three centimetres, but the entire cosmic space was there, undiminished in volume." Everything appears before his astonished eyes in a Whitmanesque enumeration: "I saw the populous sea, I saw the dawn and the evening, I saw the crowds of America, a silvery spider's web in the centre of a black pyramid, I saw a broken labyrinth (it was London), I saw eyes very close to me, unending, observing their own reflection in me as if in a mirror ..." The list continues for another page. Among the visions, Borges impossibly sees his own face and the faces of his readers—our faces—and "the atrocious remains of that which had deliciously been Beatriz Viterbo." Also, to his mortification, he sees a number of "obscene, incredible, precise letters" that the unattainable Beatriz had written to Daneri. "I was dazed and I wept," he concludes, "because my eyes had seen that secret and conjectural object whose name men usurp but that no man has ever seen: the inconceivable universe."

Once the story was finished, Borges published it in *Sur*, in the issue of September 1945. Shortly afterwards he and Estela had dinner at the Hotel Las Delicias in Adrogué, in the outskirts of Buenos Aires. This was a place of great importance to Borges. Here, as a young man, he had spent a few happy summers with his family, reading; here, a desperately unhappy thirty-five-year-old man, he attempted suicide on 25 August 1934 (an attempt he commemorated in 1978, in a story set in the future, "25 August 1983"); here he set his metaphysical detective story, "Death and the Compass," transforming Las Delicias into the beautifully named villa Triste-le-Roy. In the evening he and Estela walked through the darkened streets and Borges recited, in Italian, Beatrice's lines to Virgil, begging him to accompany Dante in his voyage through Hell. This is Dorothy L. Sayers' translation:

O courteous Mantuan soul, whose skill in song
Keeps green on earth a fame that shall not end
While motion rolls the turning sphere along!

A friend of mine, who is not Fortune's friend,
Is hard beset upon the shadowy coast ...

Estela recalled the lines and told me that Borges had made fun of the crafty flattery Beatrice used to get what she wanted. "Then Borges turned to me," Estela said, "though he could barely make me out under the misty street lamp, and asked if I would marry him."

Half amused, half serious, she told him that she might. "But Georgie, don't forget that I'm a disciple of Bernard Shaw. We can't get married unless we go to bed first." To me, across the dinner table, she added, "I knew he'd never dare."

Their relationship, such as it was, continued half-heartedly for another year. According to Estela, their break-up came through Borges's mother who, as her son's constant chaperone, had little regard for his woman friends. Later, in 1967, after his mother had apparently consented to his marriage with Elsa Astete de Millán ("I think it will be all right for you to marry Elsa, because she's a widow and she knows about life"), Estela commented, "She's found him a replacement." The marriage was, however, a disaster. Elsa, jealous of anyone for whom Borges felt affection, forbade him to visit his mother and never invited her to their flat. Elsa shared none of Borges's literary interests. She read very little. Borges enjoyed telling his dreams every morning, over coffee and toast; Elsa didn't dream, or said she didn't dream, which Borges found inconceivable. Instead she cared for the trappings that fame had brought Borges, and which he so emphatically despised. At Harvard, where Borges had been invited to lecture, she insisted that he be paid a higher fee and that they be given more luxurious accommodations. One night, one of the professors found Borges outside the residence, in slippers and pyjamas. "My wife locked me out," he explained, deeply embarrassed. The professor took Borges in for the night and the next morning confronted Elsa. "You're not the one who has to see him under the sheets," she answered. Another time, in their flat in Buenos Aires where I had gone to visit him, Borges waited for Elsa to leave the room and then asked me, in a whisper: "Tell me, is Beppo here?" Beppo was Borges's large white tomcat. I told him that he was, purring in one of the armchairs. "Thank God," Borges said, in a scene straight out of Nabokov's *Laughter in the Dark*. "She told me he'd run away. But I could hear him and I thought I was losing my mind."

Borges's escape from Elsa was decidedly inglorious. Since divorce didn't exist in Argentina, his only recourse was a legal separation. On 7 July 1970, his American translator, Norman Thomas di Giovanni, picked him up in a taxi at the National Library (where Borges had his office) and secretly accompanied him to the airport, where they caught a plane for Córdoba. In the meantime, instructed by Borges under Di Giovanni's guidance, a lawyer and three removal men rang the doorbell at Elsa's flat with a legal writ and the order to take away Borges's books. The marriage had lasted fifty-three days.

Once again, Borges felt that it was not his destiny to be happy. Literature provided consolation, but never quite enough, since it also brought back memories of each loss or failure, as he knew when he wrote the last lines of the first sonnet in the diptych "1964":

> No one loses (you repeat in vain)
> Except that which he doesn't have and never
> Had, but it isn't sufficient to be brave
> To learn the art of oblivion.
> A symbol, a rose tears you apart
> And a guitar can kill you.

Throughout his almost centenary life, Borges fell in love with patient regularity and with patient regularity his hopes came to nothing. He envied the literary alliances we encountered in our readings: the British soldier John Holden and Ameera, his Indian wife, in Kipling's "Without Benefit of Clergy" ("Since when hast thou been a slave, my queen?"), the chaste Sigurd and Brynhild from the *Völsunga Saga* (two lines of which are now engraved on his tombstone in Geneva), Stevenson and Fanny (whom Borges imagined happy), Chesterton and his wife (whom he imagined content). The long list of names of Borges's beloved can be culled from the dedications to his stories and poems: Estela Canto, Haydée Lange, María Esther Vázquez, Ulrike von Kühlmann, Silvina Bullrich, Beatriz Bibiloni Webster de Bullrich, Sara Diehl de Moreno Hueyo, Margot Guerrero, Cecilia Ingenieros—"all unique," as Bioy said, "and all irreplaceable."

One evening, over the usual colourless pasta at the restaurant of the Hotel Dora, he told me that he believed, with literary faith, in what he called "the mystery of women and the heroic destiny of men." He felt unable to recreate that mystery on the page: the few women in his short stories are cogs in the plot, not characters in their own right, except perhaps the avenging Emma Zunz, whose argument was given to him by a woman, Cecilia Ingenieros. The two rival women artists in "The Duel" (a story that properly acknowledges its debt to Henry James) are sexless except in name, and so is the old woman in "The Elderly Lady." The shared woman in "The Intruder" is little more than a thing the rival brothers have to kill in order to remain faithful to one another. The strangest of Borges's fictional women, Ulrica, in the eponymous story, is less a woman than a phantom: she, a young Norwegian student, gives herself to the elderly Colombian professor Javier

Otárola, whom she calls Sigurd, and who, in turn, calls her Brynhild. First she appears willing, then cold, and Otárola says to her, "Brynhild, you walk as if you wished a sword between the two of us." The story ends, "There was no sword between us. Time drifted away like sand. Love flowed, secular in the shadows, and I possessed for the first and last time the image of Ulrica."

Borges's men, on the other hand, fulfil their heroic destinies with stoic determination, hardly ever knowing whether they've achieved anything, a few times aware that they have failed. The dreaming magus of "The Circular Ruins," who realizes that he too is someone's dream, the laborious novelist Herbert Quain, who admits that his work belongs "not to art, but to the mere history of art," the metaphysical detective Erik Lönrrot, who goes willingly to his own death, the irredeemable Nazi Otto Dietrich zur Linde, who coins for himself the illustrious epitaph "Let Heaven exist, even though our place be in Hell," the bull-faced prisoner in the labyrinth waiting patiently for his redeemer to slay him, the playwright Jaromir Hladík, for whom God performs a secret miracle to allow him to complete a play before dying, the sedentary Juan Dahlmann, who, in "The South," is suddenly offered an epic death to crown his quiet life—all these were the men whose fate Borges felt he somehow shared. "Plato, who like all men, was unhappy ..." began one of his lectures at the University of Buenos Aires. I think Borges felt this to be the inescapable truth.

Borges had wished for a simple, uncomplicated union; fate allotted him entanglements that seemed plotted by Henry James, whose arguments, though he much admired their invention, he found at times too psychologically convoluted. His last attempt at marriage, to María Kodama, apparently took place on 26 April 1986, less than two months before his death, through a license issued *in absentia* by the mayor of a small Paraguayan town. I say apparently, because the procedures were shrouded in confusing secrecy and since Borges's marriage to Elsa had never been annulled, it would seem that in marrying María he might have been guilty of bigamy. María had been one of his students in the Anglo-Saxon courses and later, in the sixties, had begun to accompany him on his travels. Her marriage to Borges surprised most people and angered many who felt that she had deliberately distanced the old man from his friends. The truth is that Borges's friends felt jealous of anyone for whom Borges showed affection or interest, and Borges, with the wilfulness of Jehovah, allowed these jealousies to flourish.

Now, in his eighties, with María in charge, Borges no longer dined at the Bioys', no longer met with many of his old acquaintances: all this was blamed on Maria, never on Borges's mutability. No one recalled that over the years Borges had often erased a name from a poem's dedication and replaced it, in a childlike switch of affections, with that of another, more recent recipient: the new erasures were attributed to María. Even the fact of his dying in Geneva, far from his eternal Buenos Aires, was blamed on María's jealousy. A day or so before his death, Borges called Bioy from Geneva. Bioy says he sounded infinitely sad. "What are you doing in Geneva? Come home," Bioy said to him. "I can't," Borges answered. "And anyway, any place is good enough to die in." Bioy said that in spite of their friendship, he felt, as a writer, hesitant to touch such a good exit line.

But there were those—Borges's editor at Gallimard, Héctor Bianciotti, for instance, and Cortázar's widow, Aurora Bernárdez—who saw María Kodama merely as a devoted and zealous companion. According to them, Borges had met at last his adamant, jealous, remote, protective Beatrice. To Bianciotti, Borges had said: "I'm dying of cancer of the liver, and I'd like to end my days in Japan. But I don't speak Japanese, or only a few words, and I would like to be able to talk my last hours away." From Geneva, he asked Bianciotti to send him books never mentioned in his writings: the comedies of Molière, the poems of Lamartine, the works of Rémy de Gourmont. Then Bianciotti understood: they were the books Borges had told him he had read as an adolescent in Geneva. The last book he chose was Novalis's *Heinrich von Ofterdingen* which he asked the German-speaking nurse to read to him throughout the long, painful wait. The day before he died, Bianciotti came to see him and sat by his bed throughout the night, holding his old hand, until the next morning.

Borges died on 14 June 1986. Ten years later, rereading "The Aleph" for his memory's sake, I wondered where it was that I'd come across the idea of the all-encompassing space in Borges's work—Hobbes's *nunc-stans* or *hic-stans* quoted as an epigraph to "The Aleph."[1] I looked through my two shelves of Borges: the tattered original Emecé editions, cluttered with typos; the two fat volumes of the incomplete *Obras Completas* and *Obras Completas en Colaboración*, no less typo-ridden; the glossy and somewhat more prolix Alianza editions; the erratic English translations; the superb French Pléiade edition of his *Oeuvres*, so lovingly edited by Bernès that in my mind it almost supersedes the original Spanish. (Borges might not have minded: he once said of the English version of Beckford's *Vathek*, written in French, that "the original is unfaithful to the translation.")

Roger Caillois, responsible for making Borges known in France ("I'm an invention of Caillois," Borges said once) suggested that the master's central theme was the labyrinth; as if to confirm this supposition, the best-known collection of somewhat clumsily translated Borges pieces in English bears that title in the plural. Astonishingly (at least for me, who thought myself quite familiar with Borges's work) as I reread his books, I found that, far more than the labyrinth, it is the idea of an object, or a place or person or moment, that is all objects, places, persons and moments, that pervasively appears throughout his writing.

I made a list on the endpaper pages of my Pléiade volume, but I'm sure it is far from exhaustive:

It is headed by the most obvious: "The Zahir," companion piece to "The Aleph." The *zahir*, which means "visible" in Arabic, is an object (a coin, but also a tiger, an astrolabe) that once seen cannot be forgotten. Quoting Tennyson's line about the flower in the crannied wall, Borges says that "perhaps he meant that there is no event, however humble, that does not imply the history of the world and its infinite concatenation of effects and causes." Then comes the celebrated Library of Babel, "which some call the Universe" and which contains every possible book, including "the true account of my death." This infinite Library is abridged into a single book of infinitely thin pages, mentioned in a note to the story of the same name and expanded in the late "Book of Sand." The universal encyclopaedia sought by the narrator in the long story "The Congress" is not impossible: it already exists and is the universe itself, like the map of the Nation of Cartographers (in *El Hacedor*), which Lewis Carroll foresaw in *Sylvie and Bruno* and which, in Borges's short fable, coincides with the country it set out to map.

Characters too can be, like places and objects in Borges's work, all-encompassing. Sir Thomas Browne, whom Borges loved, had said it for all time: "Every man is not only himself;

there hath been many Diogenes, and as many Timons, though but few of that name: men are liv'd over again, the world is now as it was in Ages past; there was none then, but there hath been some one since that parallels him, and is, as it were, his revived self."[2] Borges rejoiced in the paragraph and asked me to read it to him several times. He approved of Browne's seemingly naive "though but few of that name," which "makes him dear to us, eh?" and chuckled without really expecting an answer. One of the earliest of these "revived selves" is Tom Castro, the unlikely impostor from *A Universal History of Infamy*, who, though a semi-idiot who speaks not a word of English, tries to pass himself off as the English-born and aristocratic Tichborne heir, following the dictum that one man is in fact all men. Other versions of this protean character are the unforgetting and unforgettable Funes (in "Funes the Memorious") whose memory is a rubbish heap of everything seen throughout his short life; the Arab philosopher Averroes (in "The Search of Averroes") who tries, across the centuries, to understand Aristotle, much like Borges himself in search of Averroes, and the reader in search of Borges; the man who has been Homer (in "The Immortal") and who has also been a sampling of all men throughout our history, and who created a man called Ulysses who calls himself Nobody; Pierre Menard who becomes Cervantes in order to write, once again but in our time, *Don Quixote*. Already in the epigraph to the early book of poems *Fervor de Buenos Aires*, published in 1923, Borges had written, "If the pages of this book consent a single happy verse, may the reader forgive me the discourtesy of having usurped it myself, previously. Our nothings are barely dissimilar; it is a trivial and fortuitous circumstance that you are the reader of these exercises, and I their author." In "Everything and Nothing" Shakespeare begs God to let him, who has been so many men, be one and himself. God confesses to Shakespeare that He too is nothing: "I dreamed the world [says God] as you dreamed your work, my Shakespeare, and among the forms of my dream are you who like Myself are many and no one." In "The Lottery of Babylon" every man has been a proconsul, every man has been a slave: that is to say, every man has been every man. My list also includes this note, with which Borges ends his review of Victor Fleming's film, *Dr. Jekyll and Mr. Hyde*: "Beyond Stevenson's dualist parable and close to the *Assembly of the Birds* composed in the twelfth century of our era by Farid ud-din Attar, we can imagine a pantheistic film whose many characters, in the end, resolve themselves into One, which is everlasting." The idea became a script written with Bioy (*The Others*) and then a film directed by Hugo Santiago.

Even in Borges's everyday talk, the theme of all-in-one was constantly present. When I saw him, briefly, after the Malvinas War had been declared, we talked, as usual, about literature and touched on the theme of the double. Borges said to me sadly, "Why do you think no one's noticed that General Galtieri and Mrs. Thatcher are one and the same person?" Another time, consoling Silvina Ocampo on the death of a favourite dog, he tried to use the Platonic tag: "You haven't lost a dog, one dog is all dogs and all dogs are your dead dog ..." Silvina told him, in no uncertain terms, what to do with his metaphysical argument.

But this multiplicity of beings and places, this invention of an eternal being and an eternal place, is not enough for happiness, which Borges considered a moral imperative, and in an apocryphal tale appended to *El Hacedor*, Borges (under the name Gaspar Camerarius) intoned his two-line long *regret d'Héraclite*:

I, who have been so many men, have never been
He in whose embrace Matilde Urbach swooned.

Four years before his death, Borges published one more book, *Nine Essays on Dante*, composed of pieces written in the forties and fifties, and revised much later. In the first paragraph of his introduction, Borges imagines an old engraving found in an imaginary Oriental library, in which everything in the world is arduously depicted. Borges suggests that Dante's poem is like that all-encompassing engraving, the *Commedia* as the Aleph.

The essays are written in Borges's slow, precise, asthmatic voice; as I turn the pages, I can hear his deliberate hesitations, the ironic questioning tone with which he liked to end his most original remarks, the solemn *recitativo* in which he would quote long passages from memory. His ninth essay on Dante, "Beatrice's Last Smile," begins with a statement that he would have made with disarming simplicity: "My purpose is to comment on the most moving verses ever achieved in literature. They are included in the thirty-first canto of *Paradiso* and, although they are famous, no one appears to have noticed the sorrow hidden in them, no one heard them fully. It is true that the tragic substance they hold belongs less to the book than to the author of the book, less to Dante the protagonist than to Dante the writer or inventor."

Borges then goes on to tell the story. High on the peak of Mount Purgatory, Dante loses sight of Virgil. Led by Beatrice, whose beauty increases as they cross each new heaven, he reaches the Empyrean. In this infinite region, things far removed are no less clearly visible than those close by ("as in a Pre-Raphaelite canvas," Borges notes). Dante sees, high above, a river of light, flocks of angels and the Rose made from the souls of the just, arranged in orderly rows. Dante turns to hear Beatrice speak of what he has seen, but his Lady has vanished. In her place, he sees the figure of a venerable old man. "And she? Where is she?" Dante cries. The old man instructs Dante to lift his eyes and there, crowned in glory, he sees her high above him, in one of the circles of the Rose, and offers her his prayer of thanks. The text then reads (in Barbara Reynolds' translation):

> Such was my prayer and she, so distant fled,
> It seemed, did smile and look on me once more,
> Then to the eternal fountain turned her head.

Borges (always the craftsman) noted that "seemed" refers to the faraway distance but horribly contaminates Beatrice's smile as well.

How can we explain these verses? Borges asks. The allegorical annotators have seen Reason (Virgil) as an instrument for reaching faith, and Faith (Beatrice) as an instrument for reaching the divinity. Both disappear once the goal is reached. "This explanation," Borges adds, "as the reader will have noticed, is no less irreproachable than it is frigid; these verses were never born from such a miserable equation."

The critic Guido Vitali (whom Borges had read) suggested that Dante, creating Paradise, was moved by a desire to found a kingdom for his Lady. "But I'd go further," Borges says. "I suspect that Dante constructed literature's best book in order to insert a few meetings with the unrecapturable Beatrice. Or rather, the circles of punishment and the southern Purgatory and the nine concentric circles and Francesca and the mermaid and the Gryphon and Bertrand de Born are inserts; a smile and a voice, which he knows lost, are what is essential."

Then Borges allows us the ghost of a confession: "That an unhappy man should imagine happiness is in no way extraordinary; all of us do so every single day. Dante too does it as we do, but something, always, allows us to glimpse the horror behind these happy fictions." He continues, "The old man points to one of the circles of the lofty Rose. There, in a halo, is Beatrice; Beatrice whose eyes used to fill him with unbearable beatitude, Beatrice who used to dress in red gowns, Beatrice of whom he had thought so much that he was astonished to consider that certain pilgrims, whom he saw one morning in Florence, had never even heard of her, Beatrice who once cut him cold, Beatrice who died at the age of twenty-four, Beatrice de Folco Portinari who had married Bardi." Dante sees her and prays to her as he would pray to God, but also as he would pray to a desired woman.

> O thou in whom my hopes securely dwell,
> And who, to bring my soul to Paradise,
> Didst leave the imprint of thy steps in Hell …

Beatrice then casts her eyes on him for a single moment and smiles, and then turns forever towards the eternal fountain of light.

And Borges concludes, "Let us retain one indisputable fact, a single and humble fact: that this scene was *imagined* by Dante. For us, it is very real; for him, it was less so. (Reality, for him, was the fact that first life and then death had snatched Beatrice away). Absent for ever from Beatrice, alone and perhaps humiliated, he imagined the scene in order to imagine himself with her. Unfortunately for him, fortunately for the centuries that would read him, his knowledge that the encounter was imaginary deformed the vision. That is why the atrocious circumstances take place—so much more infernal, of course, because they take place in the highest heaven, the Empyrean: Beatrice's disappearance, the old man who takes her place, her sudden elevation to the Rose, the fleeting smile and glance, the everlasting turning away."

I'm wary of seeing in one man's reading, however brilliant that reading might be, a reflection of his own self; as Borges would no doubt argue, in his defence of the reader's freedom to choose and to reject, not every book serves as a mirror for every one of its readers. But in the case of the *Nine Essays* I think the inference is justified, and Borges's reading of Dante's destiny helps me read that of Borges. In a short essay published in *La Prensa* in 1926, Borges himself had stated: "I've always said that the lasting aim of literature is to display our destinies."

Borges suggested that Dante wrote the *Commedia* in order to be, for a moment, with Beatrice. It isn't impossible that in some way, in order to be with a woman, *any* woman of the many he desired, to be privy to her mystery, to be more than just a wordsmith, to be or to try to be a lover and be loved for his own sake and not for that of his inventions, Borges created the Aleph, again and again, throughout his work. In that imaginary all-encompassing place where everything possible and impossible is happening, or in the arms of the man who is all men, she, the unattainable, might be his, or if she still would not be his, she would at least not be his under circumstances less painful to bear, because he himself had invented them.

But as he, the master craftsman, knew very well, the laws of invention won't bend any more easily than those of the world called real. Teodelina Villar in "The Zahir," Beatriz Viterbo in "The Aleph," don't love the intellectual narrator, Borges, who loves them. For the sake of the story, these women are unworthy

Beatrices—Teodelina is a snob, a slave to fashion "less preoccupied with beauty than with perfection"; Beatriz is a society belle obscenely infatuated with her obnoxious cousin—because, for the fiction to work, the miracle (the revelation of the Aleph, or of the memorable *zahir*) must take place among blind and unworthy mortals, the narrator included.

Borges once remarked that the destiny of the modern hero is *not* to reach Ithaca or the Holy Grail. Perhaps his sorrow, in the end, came from realizing that instead of granting him the much-longed-for and sublime erotic encounter, his craft demanded that he fail: Beatriz was not to be Beatrice, he was not to be Dante, he was to be only Borges, a fumbling dream-lover, still unable, even in his own imagination, to conjure up the one fulfilling and almost perfect woman of his waking dreams.

---

[1] Two early sources for the Aleph might be: 1) The vision of St. Benedict of Nursia who, shortly before his death c. 547, looked up from his prayers and saw in the darkness outside his window that "the whole world appeared to be gathered into one sunbeam and thus brought before his eyes." (T. F. Lindsay, *St. Benedict, His Life and Work*, London, 1949). 2) In a tale of the late-eighteenth-century Rabbi Nachman of Bratzlav, a map is described, which shows "the worlds at all times, and whatever happened stood drawn on it to read, the fate of countries, cities and men and all the pathways to this world and the hidden pathways to distant worlds. They stood each thing as it was at the hour when the world was created, as it has been since then, and as it is today." (Martin Buber, *The Tales of Rabbi Nachman*, trans. by Maurice Friedman, New York: Avon Books, 1970).

[2] Though Gerard Manley Hopkins said it perhaps more movingly:
I am all at once what Christ is ' since he was what I am, and
This Jack, joke, poor potsherd, ' patch, matchwood, immortal diamond
Is immortal diamond.
("That Nature Is a Heraclitean Fire and of the Comfort of the Resurrection").

The Death of Che Guevara

I believe in an ultimate decency of things.

ROBERT LOUIS STEVENSON,
23 August 1893

On October 8, 1967, a small battalion of Bolivian army rangers trapped a group of guerrilleros in a scrubby gully in the wilderness east of Sucre, near the village of La Higuera. Two were captured alive: a Bolivian fighter known simply as Willy and Ernesto "Che" Guevara, hero of the Cuban Revolution, leader of what Bolivia's president, General René Barrientos, called "the foreign invasion of agents of Castro-Communism." Lieutenant Colonel Andrés Selich, hearing the news, scrambled into a helicopter and flew to La Higuera. In the ramshackle schoolhouse, Selich held a forty-five-minute dialogue with his captive. Up to recently, little was known of Che's last hours; after a silence of twenty-nine years, Selich's widow finally allowed the American journalist Jon Lee Anderson to consult Selich's notes of that extraordinary conversation. Beyond their importance as a historical document, there is something poignant about the fact that a man's last words were respectfully recorded by his enemy.

"Comandante, I find you somewhat depressed," Selich said. "Can you explain the reasons why I get this impression?"

"I've failed," Che replied. "It's all over, and that's the reason why you see me in this state." ...

"Are you Cuban or Argentine?" asked Selich.

"I am Cuban, Argentine, Bolivian, Peruvian, Ecuadoran, etc.... You understand."

"What made you decide to operate in our country?"

"Can't you see the state in which the peasants live?" asked Che. "They are almost like savages, living in a state of poverty that depresses the heart, having only one room in which to sleep and cook and no clothing to wear, abandoned like animals ..."

"But the same thing happens in Cuba," retorted Selich.

"No, that's not true," Che fired back. "I don't deny that in Cuba poverty exists, but [at least] the peasants there have an illusion of progress, whereas the Bolivian lives without hope. Just as he is born, he dies, without ever seeing improvements in his human condition."

The CIA wanted Che alive, but perhaps their orders never reached the Cuban-born CIA agent Félix Rodriguez, in charge of supervising the operation. Che was executed the next day. To make it appear that their captive had been killed in battle, the executioner fired at his arms and legs. Then, as Che was writhing on the ground, "apparently biting one of his wrists in an effort to avoid crying out," one last bullet entered his chest and filled his lungs with blood. Che's body was flown to Vallegrande where it lay on view for a couple of days, observed by officials, journalists and townspeople. Selich and other officers stood at the head, posing for the photographer, before having the corpse "disappear" into a secret grave near the Vallegrande airstrip. The photographs of the dead Che, with their inevitable echo of the dead Christ (the half-naked lean body, the bearded, suffering face) became one of the essential icons of my generation, a generation that was barely ten years old when the Cuban Revolution took place in 1959.

The news of the death of Che Guevara reached me towards the end of my first and only year of university in Buenos Aires. It was a warm October (summer had started early in 1967) and my friends and I were making plans to travel south and camp in the Patagonian Andes. It was an area we knew well. We had trekked in Patagonia most summers throughout high school, led by enthusiastic left-wing monitors whose political credos ran from conservatist Stalinism to free-thinking anarchism, from melancholic Trotskyism to the Argentinian-style socialism of Alfredo Palacios, and whose book-bags, which we rifled as we sat around the campfire, included the poems of Mao Tse-tung (in the old-fashioned spelling), of Blas de Otero and Neruda, the stories of Saki and Juan Rulfo, the novels of Alejo Carpentier and Robert Louis Stevenson. A story by Cortázar that had as its epigraph a line from Che's diaries led us to discuss the ideals of the Cuban Revolution. We sang songs from the Spanish Civil War and the Italian Resistance, the rousing "Dirge of the Volga Boatmen" and the scabrous rumba "My Puchunguita Has Ample Thighs," various tangos and numerous Argentinian zambas. We were nothing if not eclectic.

Camping down south was not just an exercise in tourism. Our Patagonia was not Chatwin's. With youthful fervour, our monitors wanted to show us the hidden side of Argentinian society—a side that we, from our comfortable Buenos Aires homes, never got to see. We had a vague idea of the slums that surrounded our prosperous neighbourhoods—*villas miseria* as we called them, or "misery villages"—but we knew nothing of the slave-like conditions, like those described by Che to Selich, that still existed for many of the peasants on our country's vast estates, nor of the systematic genocide of the native people that had been officially conducted by the military until well into the thirties. With more or less earnest intentions, our monitors wanted us to see "the real Argentina."

One afternoon, near the town of Esquel, our monitors led us into a high and rocky canyon. We walked in single file, wondering where this dusty, unappealing stone corridor would lead us, when up in the canyon's walls we began to see openings, like the entrances to caves, and in the openings the gaunt, sickly faces of men, women and children. The monitors walked us through the canyon and back, never saying a word, but when we set up camp for the night they told us something of the lives of the people we had seen, who made their home in the rocks like animals, eking out a living as occasional farmhands, and whose children rarely lived beyond the age of seven. Next morning, two of my classmates asked their monitor how they could join the Communist Party. Others took a less sedate path. Several became fighters in the seventies war against the military dictatorship; one, Mario Firmenich, became the bloodthirsty *capo* of the Montoneros guerrilla movement and for years held the dubious celebrity of heading the military's most-wanted list.

The news of Che's death felt colossal and yet almost expected. For my generation, Che had incarnated the heroic social being most of us knew we could never become. The curious mix of resoluteness and recklessness that appealed so strongly to my generation, and even to the one that followed, found in Che the perfect incarnation. In our eyes he was in life already a legendary figure, whose heroism we were certain would somehow survive beyond the grave. It did not surprise us to learn that, after Che's death, Rodriguez, the treacherous CIA agent, suddenly began to suffer from asthma, as if he had inherited the dead man's malady.

Che had seen what we had seen, he had felt, as we had felt, outrage at the fundamental injustices of "the human condition," but unlike us, he had done something about it. That his methods were dubious, his political philosophy superficial, his morality ruthless, his ultimate success impossible seemed (perhaps still seems) less important than the fact that he had taken upon himself to fight against what he believed was wrong even though he was never quite certain what in its stead would be right.

Ernesto Guevara de la Serna (to give him his full name before fame reduced it to a simple "Che") was born in the city of Rosario, in Argentina, on 14 May 1928, though the birth certificate stated "June" to hide the reasons for his parents' hasty marriage. His father, whose ancestors first arrived in Argentina with the conquistadores, owned a plantation in the subtropical province of Misiones. Because of Ernesto's asthma, which plagued him throughout his life, the family moved to the more salubrious climate of Córdoba and later, in 1947, to Buenos Aires. There Ernesto studied at the faculty of medicine and, armed with a doctor's title, set off to explore the Latin-American continent "in all its terrible wonder." He was enthralled by what he saw and found it hard to give up the wandering life: from Ecuador he wrote to his mother announcing that he had become "a 100 per cent adventurer." Among the many people he met on this Grand Tour, one in particular seemed to haunt him: an old Marxist refugee from Stalin's pogroms whom Ernesto came across in Guatemala. "You will die with the fist clenched and the jaw tense," said this far-flung Tiresias, "in perfect demonstration of hate and of combat, because you are not a symbol, you are an authentic member of a society that is crumbling: the spirit of the beehive speaks through your mouth and moves in your actions; you are as useful as I, but you don't know the usefulness of the help you give to the society that sacrifices you." Ernesto could not have known that the old man had given him his epitaph.

In Guatemala, Ernesto became acutely aware of political strife, and identified for the first time with the revolutionary cause. There, and in Mexico soon afterwards, he became acquainted with the Cuban emigrés who were leading the struggle against the dictator Fulgencio Batista whose corrupt regime had so fascinated and repelled Hemingway and Graham Greene. With a canny nose for troublemakers, CIA agent David Atlee Phillips, appointed at the time to Central America, opened a file on the young Argentinian doctor—a file that over the years was to become one of the thickest in the CIA's records. In July of 1955 the first meeting between Ernesto Guevara and Fidel Castro took place in Mexico. Castro, who as far back as 1948, as a twenty-one-year-old law student, had begun plotting against Batista's regime, took an immediate liking to the Argentinian whom the other Cubans had started calling "Che" after the Argentinian colloquial address. "I think there is a mutual sympathy between us," wrote Che in his diaries. He was right.

After the triumph of the Cuban Revolution in 1959, Che sought an ambitious sequel. We don't know whether he would have lent his support, out of loyalty to the Revolution, to the tyrannical measures Castro was to take in the years to come to protect his regime. Che's sights were far in the future. After the war in Cuba, Che believed, the revolutionaries would spread to other neighbouring nations (Bolivia was the first chosen). Here they would wage war against the oligarchy and their imperialist bosses, wars that would finally force the arch-enemy, the United States, to step into the fray. As a result,

Latin America would unite against "the foreign invader," following the model of Vietnam, and defeat imperialism on the continent. Che's battle was not against all forms of power, nor was it even against the notion of a tiered society. He was certainly not an anarchist: he believed in the need for organized leadership and he imagined a pan-American state under a strong-handed but moral government. In a small book on the Greek idea of liberty, *La Grèce antique à la découverte de la liberté*, the French historian Jacqueline de Romilly pointed out that Antigone's revolt stemmed not from a rejection of authority but, on the contrary, from obedience to a moral law rather than to an arbitrary edict. Che too felt compelled to obey such moral laws and it was for them that he was willing to sacrifice everything and everyone, including, of course, himself. As we know, the events never proceeded beyond the Bolivian campaign. Whether Che ever learned what the usefulness of his sacrifice was, is a question that remains unanswered.

And yet something of Che's ideal survives beyond the political defeat, even in these days when greed has almost acquired the quality of a virtue and corporate ambition overrides mere social (let alone socialist) considerations. In part, he has become another colourful Latin American figure, like Zapata or Pancho Villa: in Bolivia, the National Tourist Board now conducts tours to the site of Che's final campaign and to the hospital where his body was displayed. But that is not all that remains. The face of Che—alive with his starred beret, or dead, staring as if his eyes could see into a point beyond our shoulder—still seems to encompass a vast and heroic view of men and women's role in the world, a role that may seem to us today utterly beyond our capabilities or our interest.

No doubt he had the *physique du rôle*. Epic literature requires an iconography. Zorro and Robin Hood (via Douglas Fairbanks and Errol Flynn) lent the live Che their features, and in the popular imagination he was a younger Don Quixote, a younger Garibaldi. Dead, as the nuns at the Vallegrande Hospital noted when they surreptitiously snipped off locks of his hair to keep inside reliquaries, he resembled the deposed Christ, dark uniformed men surrounding him like Roman soldiers in modern costume. Up to a point, the dead face superseded the live one. A notorious passage in Fernando Solanas's four-hour 1968 documentary, *The Hour of the Furnaces*, which brilliantly chronicled Argentinian history from its earliest days to the death of Che, held the camera for several minutes on that lifeless face, forcing the audience to pay visual homage to the man who carried for us our urge for action in the face of injustice, who bore for us our bothersome *agenbite of inwit*. We stare at that face and wonder: at what point did he pass from lamenting the sorrows of this world, pitying the fate of the poor and conversationally condemning the ruthless greed of those in power, to doing something about it all, taking action?

Perhaps it's possible to point to the moment in which the passage took place. On January 22, 1957, Che Guevara killed his first man. Che and his comrades were in the Cuban bush; it was midday. A soldier started shooting at them from a hut barely twenty metres from where they stood. Che fired two shots. At the second shot, the man fell. Until that moment, the earnest indignation at universal injustice had expressed itself in byronic gestures, bad verse which Che wrote with echoes of nineteenth-century bombast and the sort of academic prose known in Latin America as revolutionary, littered with the vocabulary of inaugural speeches and purple and hackneyed metaphors. After that first death something changed. Che, the ardent but conventional intellectual, became irrevocably a man of action, a destiny that had perhaps been his all along, even though everything in him seemed to conspire against his ever fulfilling it. Racked by asthma that made him stumble through long speeches, let alone long marches, conscious of the paradox of having been born into the class that benefited from the unfair system he had set out to challenge, moved suddenly to act rather than to reflect on the precise goals of his actions, Che assumed, with stubborn determination, the role of the romantic hero, and became the figure whom my generation required in order to ease our conscience.

Thoreau famously declared that "Action from principle, the perception and the performance of right, changes things and relations; it is essentially revolutionary, and does not consist wholly with anything which was. It not only divides states and churches, it divides families; ay, it divides the individual, separating the diabolical in him from the divine." Che (who, like all Argentinian intellectuals of his time, must have read *Civil Disobedience*) would have agreed with this paraphrase of Matthew 10:34–35.

Imagination to Power!

Remembering Julio Cortázar

> Anyone who doesn't read Cortázar is doomed. Not to read him is a serious invisible disease which, in time, can have terrible consequences. Something similar to a man who has never tasted peaches, he would quietly become sadder, noticeably paler, and probably, little by little, he would lose all his hair.
>
> PABLO NERUDA

IT WAS 1963. We were fifteen years old and in the third year of the Colegio Nacional de Buenos Aires, that vast, mausoleum-like building, which had, for over a century, bred politicians and intellectuals for the consumption of the state. Here we studied Argentinian history and Spanish, Latin and chemistry, the geography of Asia through long lists of rivers, lakes and mountains, and something called Hygiene, which included bits of anatomy and rudimentary sexual education. For us, it was the Age of Discovery: socialism, metaphysics, the arts of bribery and counterfeiting, friendship, surrealism, Ezra Pound, horror movies, the Beatles and sex. Under the influence of a Borges story that suggested that reality was a fiction, we went around the stores close to the school asking whether they sold *fiulsos* (a word we had just made up) and to our immense delight were told at one old haberdasher's that they didn't have any right now but would be receiving some soon. It was in this welcoming spirit that one afternoon we discovered Cortázar.

One of us had found, in the bookstore across the street from school, a small volume called *Bestiario*. It was square, the size of a shirt pocket, and the cover showed a solarized black-and-white photograph of a woman or a cat. We took turns reading the stories: a house inhabited by an elderly couple, brother and sister, is gradually taken over by unnamed invaders; two young people on a bus discover a conspiracy of passengers carrying bunches of flowers; a live tiger roams an otherwise ordinary Buenos Aires household. What these stories meant, why they were written, what allegorical or satirical meanings might have been intended, we didn't know and we didn't care; their humour corresponded exactly to our mood: absurd, irreverent, nostalgic for something that hadn't yet happened.

> I was going up in the elevator and just between the first and second floors I felt I was going to vomit up a little rabbit. I have never described this to you before, not so much, I don't think, from lack of truthfulness as that, just naturally, one is not going to explain to people at large that from time to time one vomits up a small rabbit.

We became Cortázar followers. We read the stories in *End of Game*, *The Secret Weapons*, *All Fires the Fire*. We understood exactly what he meant when he spoke of the dangers of walking an unmentionable creature through the city, of attending a play and finding ourselves suddenly on the stage, of being transported from an innocent operating table to the sacrificial altar of an ancient Aztec priest. These nightmares made sense to us; we didn't know then that they were also describing something like the soul of the times.

Cortázar was born in Brussels in 1914, of Argentinian parents, and was brought up and educated in Buenos Aires. In his early twenties, working as a teacher in the provinces, he started writing his first short stories. "House Taken Over," one of the masterpieces of fantastic literature, was published by an admiring Jorge Luis Borges in 1948 in a small municipal magazine. In 1951, during Perón's dictatorship—but explicitly not for political reasons—he moved to Paris where he lived for the rest of his life, preserving in his storytelling (an exile's privilege) a Buenos Aires that no longer existed.

So much for the biography.

When I met him, he was already a celebrated writer, the playful storyteller who shared the logic of Lewis Carroll and a surrealist humour. But he was also what the French call *un écrivain engagé*, one of the "fellow travellers" sympathetic to the revolutionary cause. In certain writers (the Mexican Juan Rulfo, the Argentinian Rodolfo Walsh) both qualities were inextricably one. Not so in the case of Cortázar.

In 1968, just after the May Revolution, during which the French students had taken over the city, I arrived in Paris and, with an introduction from the poet Alejandra Pizarnik, went to see him. The man I met was a baby-faced giant (he was almost two metres tall), immensely affable and with a grim sense of humour. Cortázar offered to guide me through the city. He showed me the archway under which Pierre Curie had been struck dead by a carriage and where Marie Curie had picked up the scattered bits of his precious brain; he took me to the Place Dauphine, the triangular opening at the tip of the Île de la Cité, which Aragon called "the sex of Paris"; he pointed out Picasso's bust of Apollinaire across from the Café Bonaparte; he suggested I take his picture in front of his favourite May '68 graffiti: "*L'imagination au pouvoir*," "Imagination to Power."

Five years before our meeting, in 1963, he had published *Hopscotch*, the novel through which, Mario Vargas Llosa declared, Latin American writers "learned that literature was an inspired way of enjoying ourselves, that it was possible to explore the secrets of the world and of language while having a great time and that, while playing, one could explore mysterious levels of life hidden to our rational mind, to our logical intelligence, chasms of experience into which no one can look without serious risks, such as madness or death." As most readers now know (even those who have never read the novel) *Hopscotch* gives us explicit permission to go through the story following whatever sequence of chapters we choose; Cortázar suggests one sequence (not the one in which the book is arranged) as if to imply that by once ignoring the hierarchy of chapters imposed by the novelist, the reader makes all other combinations possible. A precursor of Cortázar's game was *Museum of the Eternal Novel* by Borges's mentor, Macedonio Fernández, which offers the reader a number of forewords and first chapters, and no ending. "My readers," Fernández had declared, "are the readers of beginnings—that is to say, the perfect readers." Another precursor might have been Borges's story, "An Examination of the Work of Herbert Quain," in which the reader is invited to follow not a random sequence of chapters but a series of novels, each of which chooses a different possibility stemming from the same plot. In each of these cases, what matters is the reader's illusion of intellectual freedom (which Laurence Sterne, the master of them all, had proposed in *Tristam Shandy*). The computer games of hypertext continue and enhance this illusion.

But while Cortázar was pursuing these literary games, he was also attempting to respond to the political struggles in Latin America. Cuba's Revolution had seemed a promise to most artists and intellectuals, and Cortázar—in spite of the warnings from Cubans exiled in Paris—gave Castro his support. For Cortázar, voluntarily distanced from the place he still called home, an artistic response didn't seem enough; a political response was required, a *prise de position*, a badge of allegiance. Rather than write the fantastic tales for which he had become famous, he attempted a more realistic, even documentary form of writing—and failed. Those accusatory stories and his novel *A Manual for Manuel* founder in spite of (or because of) these good intentions. Cortázar himself was well aware of the dangers of a literature written from a sense of duty. Speaking in 1962 to a Cuban audience in Havana, he said that he fervently believed in the future of Cuba's literature.

> But this literature will not have been written through obligation, following the slogans of the day. Its themes will be born only when their time has come, when the writer feels the need to fashion them into stories or novels, poems or plays. Its themes will then carry a deep and true-ringing message because they won't have been chosen for didactic or proselytizing reasons; they will have been chosen because an irresistible force will have struck the writer who, calling on all the resources of his art and craft, without sacrificing anything to anyone, will transmit this force to the reader, in the manner in which all essential things are

transmitted: from blood to blood, hand to hand, human being to human being.

Then, all of a sudden, in the late seventies, Cortázar, still faithful to his old political beliefs but disillusioned with the possibility of rendering these in literary terms, "without sacrificing anything to anyone," returned to his fantastic writing in his final book, *Unreasonable Hours*. Magically, a number of these stories—"Tara," "The School at Night," above all the masterful "Nightmare"—turned out to be not only brilliant examples of Cortázar at his fantastic best, but also among the most powerful political stories written in Spanish in those years—years especially noted for the literature of outrage sparked by the military dictatorships throughout Latin America. In "Tara," a group of guerrilleros has sought refuge from the military in a poor, faraway village, and their leader finds in the word games he likes to play the revelation that will allow him, before his death, to understand the evil he has been fighting. "The School at Night" follows the venerable tradition of a hero's cautionary descent to the underworld, where, among the horrors, he is given to see the dreadful times to come. "Nightmare," perhaps the last story Cortázar wrote, is in many ways a companion piece to "House Taken Over," only that here the invading presence is in the mind of a comatose woman while the outsiders—her family—can only witness the invasion from the wings. The moment of understanding overlaps with that of final destruction, when the unconscious woman's vision coincides with an assault from the real world. Anyone familiar with the report on Argentina's "disappeared" (published under the title *Nunca Más*) will understand exactly the overlapping of the two atrocious ends.

What will Cortázar be remembered for? I venture to suggest that, like one of his own characters, he will undergo a metamorphosis. The common reality that attached itself to him like a second skin—the political struggles, the difficult affairs of the heart, the messy business of literature with its passion for novelty and gossip—will quietly fade and what will remain is the shining teller of uncanny tales, tales that hold a delicate balance between the unspeakable and that which must be told, between the daily horrors of which we appear to be capable and the magical events with which we are gifted every night in the labyrinthine recesses of the mind.

IV

SEX

The Knight looked surprised at the question. "What does it matter where my body happens to be?" he said. "My mind goes on working all the same. In fact, the more head downwards I am, the more I keep inventing new things."

Through the Looking-Glass, Chapter VIII

The Gates of Paradise

"Come, we shall have some fun now!" thought Alice.

Alice's Adventures in Wonderland, Chapter VII

ONE OF THE OLDEST VERSIONS of Beauty and the Beast, told in Latin by Apuleius sometime in the second century, is the story of a princess ordered by an oracle to become the wife of a dragon. Fearing for her life, dressed in mourning, abandoned by her family, she waited at the top of a mountain for her winged husband. The monster never came. Instead, a breeze lifted her and bore her down into a peaceful valley, in which stood a house of gold and silver. Disembodied voices welcomed her, and offered her food and drink, and sang to her. When night fell, no lights were lit and in the darkness she felt someone near her. "I am your lover and your husband," a voice said, and mysteriously she was no longer afraid. The princess lived with her unseen spouse for many days.

One evening, the voices told her that her sisters were approaching the house, searching for her, and she felt a great desire to see them once again and tell them of the wonderful things that had taken place. The voices warned her not to go but her longing was too great. Crying out their names, she hurried to meet them. At first the sisters seemed overjoyed, but when they heard her story they cried and called her a fool for allowing herself to be deceived by a husband who required the cover of darkness. "There must be something monstrous about him, if he will not show himself to you in the light," they said, and felt pity for her.

That night, steeling herself for a hideous revelation, the princess lit an oil lamp and crept to where her husband was sleeping. What she saw was not a dragon, but a young man of extraordinary beauty, breathing softly into the pillow. Overjoyed, she was about to extinguish the lamp, when a drop of hot oil fell on the sleeper's left shoulder. He awoke, saw the light, said not a word, and fled.

Eros vanishes when Psyche tries to perceive him.

As an adolescent, reading about Eros and Psyche one hot afternoon at home in Buenos Aires, I didn't believe in the moral of the story. I was convinced that in my father's almost unused library, where I had found so many secret pleasures, I would find, by magic chance, the startling and unspoken thing that crept into my dreams and was the butt of schoolyard jokes. I wasn't disappointed. I glimpsed Eros through the chiffonnerie of *Forever Amber*, in a tattered translation of *Peyton Place*, in certain poems of García Lorca, in the sleeping-car chapter of Moravia's *The Conformist* which I read haltingly at thirteen, in Roger Peyrefitte's *Particular Friendships*.

And Eros didn't vanish.

When a couple of years later I was able to compare my readings to the actual sensation of my hand brushing for the first time over my lover's body, I had to admit that, for once, literature had fallen short. And yet the thrill of those forbidden pages remained. The panting adjectives, the brazen verbs, were perhaps not useful to describe my own confused emotions, but they conveyed to me, then and there, something brave and astonishing and unique.

This uniqueness, I was to discover, brands all our essential experiences. "We live together, we act on, and react to, one another," wrote Aldous Huxley in *The Doors of Perception*, "but always and in all circumstances we are by ourselves. The martyrs go hand in hand into the arena; they are crucified alone. Embraced, the lovers desperately try to fuse their insulated ecstasies into a single self-transcendence; in vain. By its very nature every embodied spirit is doomed to suffer and enjoy in solitude." Even in the moment of greatest intimacy, the erotic act is a solitary act.

Throughout the ages, writers have attempted to make this solitude a shared one. Through ponderous hierarchies (essays on gender etiquette, texts of medieval love-courts), through mechanics (lovemaking manuals, anthropological studies), through examples (fables, narratives of one kind or another), every culture has sought to comprehend the erotic experience in the hope that perhaps, if it is faithfully depicted in words, the reader may be able to relive it or even learn it, in the same way that we expect a certain object to preserve a memory or a monument to bring the dead to life.

It's amazing to think how distinguished a universal library of this wishful erotic literature would be. It would include, I imagine, the Platonic dialogues of ancient Greece in which Socrates discusses the types and merits of love; Ovid's *Ars Amatoria* of Imperial Rome in which Eros is considered a social function, like table manners; the *Song of Songs*, in which the loves of King Solomon and the black Queen of Sheba become reflections of the world around them, the Hindu *Kamasutra* and the *Kalyana Malla*, in which pleasure is regarded as an element of ethics; the Arcipreste de Hita's *Book of Loving Well* in fourteenth-century Spain, which pretends to draw its wisdom from popular sources; the fifteenth-century *Perfumed*

Garden of Sheik al-Nefzawi, which codifies the erotic acts according to Muslim law; the German *Minnereden* or medieval amatory discourses, in which love, like politics, is given its own rhetoric; and poetic allegories such as the *Roman de la Rose* in France and *The Faerie Queene* in England, in which the abstract noun "Love" acquires once again, as Eros had, a human or divine face.

There would be other, even stranger works, in this ideal library: the ten-volume novel *Clélie* (1654–60) by Mademoiselle de Scudéry, which includes the *Carte de Tendre*, a map charting the erotic course with its rewards and perils; the writings of the Marquis de Sade who, in tedious catalogues, noted the sexual variations to which a human group can be subjected; the theoretical books of his near-contemporary Charles Fourier, who devised entire utopian societies centred around the sexual activities of its citizens; the intimate journals of Giacomo Casanova, Ihara Saikaku, Benvenuto Cellini, Frank Harris, Anaïs Nin, Henry Miller, John Rechy, all of whom tried to recapture Eros in autobiographical memoirs.

Curled up in an armchair in my father's library, and in other, later armchairs in more houses than I care to remember, I found that Eros kept appearing in all sorts of unexpected places. In spite of the singular nature of the experiences hinted at or described on the private page, these stories touched me, aroused me, whispered secrets to me.

We may not share experiences, but we can share symbols. Transported into another realm, distracted from its subject, erotic writing at times achieves something of that essentially private act, as when the swoons and agonies of erotic desire become a vast metaphorical vocabulary for the mystical encounter. I remember the excitement with which I read, for the first time, the erotic union described by St. John of the Cross. This is Roy Campbell's translation:

> Oh night that was my guide!
> Oh darkness dearer than the morning's pride,
> Oh night that joined the lover
> To the beloved bride
> Transfiguring them each into the other.
>
> Lost to myself I stayed
> My face upon my lover having laid
> From all endeavour ceasing:
> And all my cares releasing
> Threw them amongst the lilies there to fade.

And then John Donne, for whom the erotic/mystical act is also an act of geographical exploration:

> License my roving hands and let them go,
> Before, behind, between, above, below.
> O my America! my new-found-land.

In Shakespeare's time, the erotic borrowing of the geographical vocabulary had become sufficiently common to be parodied. In the *Comedy of Errors* the slave Dromio of Syracuse describes to his master the dubious charms of the wench lusting after him—"she is spherical, like a globe; I could find out countries in her"—and proceeds to discover Ireland in her buttocks, Scotland in the barren palm of her hand, America upon her nose, "all o'er embellished with rubies, carbuncles, sapphires, declining their rich aspect to the hot breath of Spain."

William Cartwright, the nebulous seventeenth-century author of *The Royal Slave* (a play that once received praise from both Charles I and Ben Jonson), deserves to be better remembered for the following lines, which return spiritual love to its authentic source:

I was that silly thing that once was wrought
To Practise this thin Love;
I climb'd from Sex to Soul, from Soul to Thought;
But thinking there to move,
Headlong I rowl'd from Thought to Soul, and then
From Soul I lighted at the Sex agen.

Occasionally, in my haphazard reading, I found that a single image could make a poem successful. These are lines composed by a Sumerian poet *circa* 1700 B.C. She writes:

Going to my young husband—
I'll become the apple
clinging to the bough,
surrounding the stem
with my sweet flesh.

In a few cases, all that is required is an absence of description to convey the erotic power of that which has been lost. An anonymous English poet wrote this most famous of quatrains sometime in the late Middle Ages:

Western wind, when will thou blow,
The small rain down can rain?
Christ, that my love were in my arms,
And I in my bed again.

Fiction is another matter.

Of all the erotic literary genres, fiction, I think, has the hardest time of it. To tell an erotic story, a story whose subject is outside words and outside time, seems not only a futile task but an impossible one. It may be argued that any subject, in its sheer complexity or simplicity, makes its own telling impossible; that a chair or a cloud or a childhood memory are just as ineffable, just as indescribable, as lovemaking, as a dream, as music.

Not so.

We have, in most languages, a varied and rich vocabulary that conveys reasonably well, in the hands of an experienced craftsperson, the actions and the elements with which society is comfortable, the daily bric-à-brac of its political animals. But that which society fears or fails to understand, that which forced me to keep a wary eye on the door of my father's library, that which becomes forbidden, even unmentionable in public, is given no proper words with which to approach it. "To write a dream, which shall resemble the real course of a dream, with all its inconsistency, its eccentricities and aimlessness," complained Nathaniel Hawthorne in his *American Notebooks*, "up to this old age of the world, no such thing has ever been written." He could have said the same of the erotic act.

The English language in particular makes things difficult by simply not having an erotic vocabulary. The sexual organs, the sexual acts, borrow the words to define them from either the science of biology or the lexicon of vituperation. Clinical or coarse, the words to describe the marvels of physical beauty and the exultation of pleasure condemn, asepticise or deride that which should be celebrated in wonder. Spanish, German, Italian, and Portuguese suffer from this same weakness. French is, perhaps, a little more fortunate. *Baiser* for copulate, which borrows its semantics from the word "kiss"; *verge* for penis, the same word for "birch," which in its association with "trees" gives *verger* or "orchard"; *petite mort*, "little death," for the moment of ecstasy after achieving orgasm, in which the diminutive endearment takes the eternity out of dying, but retains the sense of blissfully leaving this world—have little of the nudge-nudge wink-wink quality of "fuck," "prick," and "come." The vagina (surprise, surprise) receives in French as little respect as it does in English, and *con* is hardly better than "cunt." To write an erotic story in English, or to translate one into English, requires from the writer new and crafty ways of making use of the medium, so that the reader is led, against the grain of meaning or through an entirely separate imagination of language, into an experience that society has decreed will remain unspoken. "We have placed sex," said the wise Montaigne, "in the precincts of silence."

But why have we decided that Psyche mustn't look upon Eros?

In the Judeo-Christian world, the banning of Eros finds its canonical voice in St. Augustine, a voice that echoes through the entire Middle Ages and still rings, distorted, in the censor boardrooms of our day. After a youth of womanizing and carousing (to make use of these fine preacherly words), looking back on his quest for a happy life, Augustine concludes that ultimate happiness, *eudaemonia*, cannot be achieved unless we subordinate the body to the spirit, and the spirit to God. Bodily love, *eros*, is infamous, and only *amor*, spiritual love, can lead to the enjoyment of God, to *agape*, the feast of love itself that transcends both human body and spirit. Two centuries after Augustine, St. Maximus of Constantinople put it in these words: "Love is that good disposition of the soul in which it prefers nothing that exists to knowledge of God. But no man can come to such a state of love if he be attached to anything earthly. Love," concludes St. Maximus, "is born from lack of erotic passion." This is a far cry from Plato's contemporaries, who saw Eros as the binding force (in a real physical sense) that keeps the universe together.

Condemnation of erotic passion, of the flesh itself, allows most patriarchal societies to brand Woman as the temptress, as Mother Eve, guilty of Adam's daily fall. Because she is to blame, man has a natural right to rule over her, and any deviance from this law—by woman or by man—is punishable as treacherous and sinful. An entire apparatus of censorship is constructed to protect male-defined heterosexual stereotypes and, as a result, misogyny and homophobia are both justified and encouraged by assigning women and homosexuals restricted and depreciated roles. (And children: we excise the sexuality of children from social life, while allowing it to appear in seemingly innocuous guises on the screen and in the fashion pages—as Graham Greene noted when he reviewed the films of Shirley Temple.)

Pornography requires this double standard. In pornography, the erotic must not be an integral part of a world in which both men and women, homosexual and heterosexual, seek a deeper comprehension of themselves and of the other. To be pornographic, the erotic must be amputated from its context and adhere to strict clinical definitions of that which is condemned. Pornography must faithfully embrace official normality in order to contravene it for no other purpose than immediate arousal. Pornography—or "licentiousness," as it was called—cannot exist without these official standards. "Licentious," meaning "sexually immoral," comes from "licence," permission granted (to depart from the rules). That is why our societies allow pornography, which embraces official notions of "normal" or "decent" behaviour, to exist in specific contexts, but zealously persecute artistic erotic expressions in which the authority of those in power is brought implicitly into question. "Girlie" magazines could be bought in neat brown paper bags while *Ulysses* was being tried on charges of obscenity; hard-core porno films are shown in theatres a few steps away from others at which *The Last Temptation of Christ* or *How to Make Love to a Negro* are being picketed.

Erotic literature is subversive; pornography is not. Pornography, in fact, is reactionary, opposed to change. "In pornographic novels," says Nabokov in his post-scriptum to *Lolita*, "action has to be limited to the copulation of clichés. Style, structure, imagery should never distract the reader from his tepid lust." Pornography follows the conventions of all dogmatic literature—religious tracts, political bombast, commercial advertising. Erotic literature, if it is to be successful, must establish new conventions, lend the words of the society that condemns it new meaning, and inform its readers of a knowledge that in its very nature must remain intimate. This exploration of the world from a central and utterly private place gives erotic literature its formidable power.

For the mystic, the whole universe is one erotic object, and the whole body the subject of erotic pleasure. The same can be said of every human being who discovers that not only penis and clitoris are places of pleasure but also the hands, the anus, the mouth, the hair, the soles of the feet, every inch of our astounding bodies. That which physically and mentally excites the senses and opens for us what William Blake called the Gates of Paradise, is always something mysterious and, as we all eventually find out, its shape is dictated by laws of which we know nothing. We admit to loving a woman, a man, a child. Why not a gazelle, a stone, a shoe, the sky at night?

In D. H. Lawrence's *Women in Love*, Rupert Birkin's object of desire is the vegetation itself:

> To lie down and roll in the sticky, cool young hyacinths, to lie on one's belly and cover one's back with handfuls of fine wet grass, soft as a breath, soft and more delicate and more beautiful than the touch of any woman; and then to sting one's thigh against the living dark bristles of the fir-boughs; and then to feel the light whip of the hazel on one's shoulders, stinging, and then to clasp the silvery birch-trunk against one's breast, its smoothness, its hardness, its vital knots and ridges—this was good, this was all very good, very satisfying.

In John Collier's *His Monkey Wife*, Eros is a chimp called Emily with whom an English schoolmaster, Mr. Fatigay, falls madly in love:

> "Emily!" he said. "My Angel! My Own! My Love!"
>
> At this last word, Emily raised her eyes, and extended to him her hand.
>
> Under her long and scanty hair he caught glimpses of a plum-blue skin. Into the depths of those all-dark lustrous eyes, his spirit slid with no sound of splash. She uttered a few low words, rapidly, in her native tongue. The candle, guttering beside the bed, was strangled in the grasp of prehensile foot, and the darkness received, like a ripple in velvet, the final happy sigh.

In Cynthia Ozick's "The Pagan Rabbi," Eros is a tree:

> I busied my fingers in the interstices of the bark's cuneiform. Then with forehead flat on the tree, I embraced it with both arms to measure it. My hands united on the other side. It was a young narrow weed, I did not know of what family. I reached to the lowest branch and plucked a leaf and made my tongue marvel meditatively along its periphery to assess its shape: oak. The taste was sticky and exaltingly bitter. I then placed one hand (the other I kept around the tree's waist, as it were) in the bifurcation (disgustingly termed crotch) of that lowest limb and the elegant and devoutly firm torso, and caressed that miraculous juncture with a certain languor, which gradually changed to vigor.

This is Marian Engel describing an amorous encounter between a woman and a beast in *Bear*:

> He licked. He probed. She might have been a flea he was searching for. He licked her nipples stiff and scoured her navel. With little nickerings she moved him south.
>
> She swung her hips and made it easy for him.
>
> "Bear, bear," she whispered, playing with his ears. The tongue that was muscular but also capable of lengthening itself like an eel found all her secret places. And like no human being she had ever known it persevered in her pleasure. When she came, she whimpered, and the bear licked away her tears.

And the English writer J. R. Ackerley describes in these words his love for his dog, Tulip:

> I go to bed early to end the dismal day, but she is instantly beside me, sitting upright against my pillow, her back turned,

> shifting, licking, panting, shifting, peering at my face, pulling at my arm. Sweet creature, what am I doing to you? I stretch out my hand in the gloom and stroke the small nipples ... Panting, she slackly sits while my hand caresses her, her ears flattened, her head dropped, gazing with vacant eyes into the night beyond the windows. Gradually, she relaxes, subsides. Gradually, my hand upon her, she sleeps ...

Even the lover's severed head can become an erotic object, as when Stendhal has Mathilde, in *The Red and the Black*, seek out Julien's remains:

> He heard Mathilde move hurriedly around the room. She was lighting a number of candles. When Fouque gathered enough strength to look, he saw that she had placed in front of her, on a little marble table, Julien's head, and was kissing its brow ...

Confronted with the task of making art out of a bewildering variety of objects and subjects, acts and variations, feelings and fears; limited by a vocabulary specifically designed for other purposes; walking the perilous edge between pornography and sentimentality, biology and purple prose, the coy and the over-explicit; threatened by societies intent on preserving the aristocracies of established power through the censoring forces of politics, education and religion, it is a miracle that erotic literature has not only survived this long but become braver, brighter, more confident, pursuing a multicoloured infinity of objects of desire.

A postscript: I believe that, like the erotic act, the act of reading should ultimately be anonymous. We should be able to enter the book or the bed like Alice entering the Looking-Glass Wood, no longer carrying with us the prejudices of our past, and relinquishing for that instant of intercourse our social trappings. Reading or making love, we should be able to lose ourselves in the other, into whom—to borrow St. John's image—we are transformed: reader into writer into reader, lover into lover into lover. *Jouir de la lecture*, "to enjoy reading," say the French, for whom reaching orgasm and deriving pleasure are both expressed in a single common word.

Browsing in the Rag-and-Bone Shop

What pornography is really about, ultimately, isn't sex but death.

SUSAN SONTAG

ONE SATURDAY AFTERNOON, some time ago, a friend dropped by to see me and said I looked horribly sick. I told her I *felt* horribly sick. As far as I could remember, I had only felt like this once before, after seeing a dog hit by a car. My friend asked me what had happened. I told her I had just finished reading Bret Easton Ellis's book, *American Psycho*.

The circumstances leading to this book's publication are well known. Ellis had published two novels, of which one at least, *Less Than Zero*, became a sizeable best-seller. The American publisher Simon & Schuster bought *American Psycho* for an advance of $300,000, typeset it and, at the eleventh hour (due, some say, to protests within the company by several of its editors), decided not to publish it. It was immediately picked up by Sonny Mehta of the Random House Group of Publishers, and included in the prestigious Vintage Contemporaries, a series that boasts, among many others, writers of the stature of Don DeLillo and Richard Ford. The National Organization of Women in America threatened to boycott all of Random House's books—except those by feminist authors. As a prank, *Spy* magazine sent out sections of *American Psycho* to porn magazines such as *Hustler* and *Penthouse*, all of whom turned it down on the grounds that the scenes depicted were too violent. Canada Customs tried to prevent the book from crossing the border: fortunately, they were unsuccessful. I would march in the streets for Ellis's right to have his book on the market. I would also march in the streets for my right to argue against its literary pretensions.

American Psycho follows the daily routine of one Patrick Bateman, New York businessman, young, rich and psychotic. For endless pages, Bateman sits and talks to his acquaintances (he has no friends) about brand names—of food, of clothes, of gadgets, of anything consumable—after which, without ever changing from Bateman to Mr. Hyde, he takes up murder. Though he also murders dogs, vagrants and children, Bateman's victims are usually women, whom he slowly tortures and then dismembers and devours, in scenes written by Ellis in clumsy detail.

Of course, *American Psycho* is not an isolated example. Books of this kind exist—usually under the graphic label of "splatter punk" (in the axe-murder tradition) or "hardcore thrillers" (heirs of Mickey Spillane)—but most of the time they are presented to the public in lurid covers that make no attempt to conceal the sort of story they are offering.

The packaging of *American Psycho* is a curious affair. The cover of the first edition shows a photo from *Vogue*, the face of a Robert Redford lookalike. The epigraphs quote Dostoevsky (*Notes from Underground*) regarding the need to portray in fiction certain characters who "exist in our society," Miss Manners on restraint ("If we followed every impulse, we'd be killing one another"), and the rock group Talking Heads ("And as things fell apart/ Nobody paid much attention"). The first line in the book is Dante's motto for the gates of Hell: "Abandon all hope ye who enter here." In fact everything is set up in such a way as to make the reader believe that the story that follows is indeed of a literary nature: contemporary and ironic (cover and Miss Manners quote), hip (Talking Heads), serious and philosophical (Dostoevsky and Dante).

The next 128 pages (the first brutal scene begins on page 129) are agonizing for anyone not accustomed to reading fashion advertising: "He's wearing a linen suit by Canali Milano, a cotton shirt by Ike Behar, a silk tie by Bill Blass and cap-toed leather lace-ups from Brooks Brothers. I'm wearing a lightweight linen suit with pleated trousers, a cotton shirt, a dotted silk tie, all by Valentino Couture, and perforated cap-toe leather shoes by Allen-Edmonds." This might be meant to read as social satire; it cannot be read as such because Ellis's prose does nothing except copy the model it is supposed to denounce. It is not writing; it is a stringing together of words for the purpose of compiling a catalogue.

When the gruesome scenes do occur, Ellis uses the brand-name-dropping to remind the reader that the "satiric mode" has not been abandoned. The stomach of a slaughtered woman is compared to "the eggplant and goat cheese lasagna at Il Marlibro"; the screams of a tortured woman are drowned in a Ralph Lauren camel-hair coat; the horrors are filmed with a "Sony palm-sized Handycam." Women, the main target of Bateman's frenzies, are treated much like the brand-name goods that make up his life and his language. But the point is lost in the grotesquerie of the accounts and in Ellis's awkward, flat prose. I cannot conceive how anyone is able to call this sort of writing "witty," although that is how the publishers' catalogue describes it. "*American Psycho*," reads the blurb, "is an explosive novel which brilliantly exposes American culture today in a witty but dangerously alarming way." "Alarming"? Indeed, but this quality comes not from the writing but from the fact that publishers of literary works have chosen to include a sampling of violent pornography in their lists and dressed it up as literature. Because, in however many ways I have tried to read this book, the feebleness of its style, its meagre vocabulary, and the poor craft with which the author constructs both dialogue and description disallow any approach except that of a pornographer. By this I mean that unless you, as a reader, are titillated by the scenes of violence in this book, the only other reaction you can expect is horror: not intellectual terror that would compel you to question the universe, but a merely physical horror—a revulsion not of the senses but of the gut, like that produced by shoving one's fingers down one's throat. Ann Radcliffe, author of one of the earliest Gothic novels, cleverly distinguished between terror, which dilates the soul and excites an intense activity in all our senses, and horror, which contracts them, freezes them, somehow destroys them. *American Psycho* is a novel of pornographic horror.

Of course, the literatures of terror and horror are as old as our imagination. We, as a species, don't want contentment, we shy from appeasement, we are less interested in the bud than in the worm. Death and the suffering unto death are among our most treasured readings since the first babblings of literature. It is as if, confident in the magical powers of the word, we have always expected a writer to bring to life on the page our worst nightmares, to be the geographer of an undiscovered country, to allow us through rhyme and reason vicariously to experience that which we thought unthinkable. For centuries, the writer has been, like Virgil to Dante, a guide through the foulest corners of our human imagination.

In the Western world, this guiding took place at different times under different guises. Voyages to the underworld in the literature of Greece and Rome, illustrated with frightful portraits of Hell's ghostly inhabitants; hagiography in the Middle Ages, full of detailed accounts of the tortures suffered by the martyred saints; tragedies in the Elizabethan and Jacobean eras, in which infanticide, cannibalism and rape are commonplace; the Gothic novel in the eighteenth and nineteenth centuries, with its vampirism and necrophilia—there is no doubt that horror has been part of our literary tradition. But it wasn't until 1773, with two essays published in London by J. and A. L. Aikin, that literary terror received academic recognition in its own right. "On the Pleasure derived from Objects of Terror" and "Enquiry into those kinds of Distress which excite agreeable sensations" sought to explain and affirm the proliferation of ruins, corpses, dark shadows and foul creatures that had invaded the fiction and poetry of Romantic Europe, but in fact lent aesthetic validity to all its illustrious predecessors. And about the same time a German, Friedrich von Hardenberg, better known as Novalis, made a bold discovery about the cruel appeal of terror: "It is startling," he wrote, "that the veritable source of cruelty should be desire." But desire for what?

Another contemporary, Donatien Alphonse Francois Marquis de Sade, provided a possible answer: desire to refuse civilization, to become a "child of nature," to embrace the natural order. "Cruelty," wrote Sade, "far from being a vice, is the earliest sentiment wrought in us by Nature; the infant breaks his rattle, bites his nurse's teat, strangles his pet bird, long before he has attained the age of reason." A son of the French Revolution, Sade replaced the God of Abraham ("the idea of God is the only mistake I cannot forgive my fellow men") not with the Goddess Reason but with Nature—another, more savage deity. Human passions are, for Sade, nothing but "the means employed by Nature to fulfil its designs." Nature hurls us blindly in a vertiginous progress from birth to death, establishing an order in which we are but parts of an atrocious machine that ultimately destroys us; consequently, Sade's monstrous sexual inventions appear as mechanical and unemotional devices, meticulously described less for titillation than for clinical instruction. Roland Barthes, in a controversial essay, denies that Sade is erotic because "eroticism can only be defined by a language that is perpetually allusive," and suggests that this quest for the explicit natural order, even within the debauchery, dominates the entire Sadean oeuvre.

Sade's protagonists seek the terrors of cruelty through a desire for natural order. Others, such as Poe, Kafka, the surrealists, sought disorder, taking things apart in the hope of revealing universal mysteries, like children dissecting a clockwork toy. Cruelty—for instance, the eye sliced with a razor in the archetypical surrealist film, *Un Chien Andalou*—is born from the voluptuous desire for anarchy.

These frameworks, these contexts, these notions that allow us to read depictions of horrific acts as illustrations of aesthetic or philosophical theories, are absent in Ellis's book. In Sade, in Poe, in hundreds of other writers, there are sections which, read on their own (the equivalent of what, in school, we used to call "the dirty bits") can be either titillating or revolting, or both, depending on our inclinations, but which as part of a whole acquire a different meaning. When Ovid's Marsyas is flayed alive in the *Metamorphoses*, when Lucan's witch in *The Civil Wars* bites the tongue of the corpse she has been kissing, when Lady Macbeth speaks of plucking her nipple from her baby's boneless gums and dashing its brains out, when Kafka's prisoner in "The Penal Colony" is slowly tortured to death by a needle that engraves on his body the unuttered nature of his crime, when Winston in Orwell's *1984* is threatened with rats that will attack his eyes and shouts, "Do it to Julia! Tear her face off, strip her to the bones!" when Dr. Noyes rapes his daughter-in-law with a unicorn's horn in Timothy Findley's *Not Wanted on the Voyage*—even though it may be possible for a reader to find pornography in the description by ignoring the context, that context does exist: it colours the violence, gives it meaning, allows for redemption, helps understanding. Violence, and the glimpse it gives us of Hell, is the starting point Yeats perhaps had in mind when he wrote in "The Circus Animals' Desertion," his poem on the sources of inspiration:

> I must lie down where all the ladders start,
> In the foul rag-and-bone shop of the heart.

The rag-and-bone shop is a reality, and different writers have visited it with more or less talent. Many fail, but lack of talent is not a criminal offence and badly written books will always be with us to test our charity. As regards publishers and false advertising, the peddling of one book under the cover of another is nothing but an ethical crime, and it is for such occasions that we are lumbered with a conscience. It is we, the readers, who have the final responsibility. The most astounding aspect of language is its versatility: it can be babble, it can be invective, it can be prayer, it can be joke, it can be fable. It can be revelation and exalt us, or it can be pornography and immure us. And it can't hurt to remember that every time we choose a book for bedtime, we're also picking our way through intimations of Heaven and promises of Hell.

V

WORDPLAY

"The question is," said Alice, "whether you *can* make words mean so many different things."

"The question is," said Humpty Dumpty, "which is to be master—that's all."

Through the Looking-Glass, Chapter VI

The Blind Photographer

"Can *you* keep from crying by considering things?" she asked.

"That's the way it's done," the Queen said with great decision: "nobody can do two things at once, you know."

Through the Looking-Glass, Chapter v

IN SEPTEMBER OF 1963, Seix-Barral in Barcelona published a short novel, *La ciudad y los perros* (translated into English as *The Time of the Hero*), by a young, unknown Peruvian writer, Mario Vargas Llosa. The novel reached us in Buenos Aires before the end of term. My Spanish high-school teacher said privately that it was a masterpiece and publicly that it should never be taught to a class of panting adolescents: too much rebellious violence, too much sexual darkness, too much questioning of authority. There had been nothing like it in Spanish-language fiction before. A fierce indictment of Peru's military system, incandescent with rage against the hypocrisy of the established order as mirrored in Lima's most prestigious military academy (which the author had attended), it was also the chronicle of an adolescent rite of passage into the ranks of the commanding patriarchy. The book so incensed the authorities that, in the tradition of the city's founding fathers, they ordered an *auto-da-fé* and had dozens of copies burned in the academy's courtyard. At the beginning of what was to be called, by clever cultural advertisers, the "boom" of Latin-American literature, *The Time of the Hero* was quickly recognized as a modern classic, a novel that managed to voice, in superb prose, a contagious protest while at the same time remaining wisely ambiguous, both in style and structure, through the shifting voices of its characters and the author's refusal to give the story over to the thriller genre, which it seemed to be courting.

Until then, the so-called "novel of protest" in the literatures of Latin America had held Zola as its model. Under the large shadow of the author of *La Terre* and *Germinal*, the Ecuadoran Jorge Icaza had written *Huasipungo*, the Peruvian Ciro Alegría, *El mundo es ancho y ajeno*—novels concerned with the plight of the exploited Indians, but novels whose craft, unfortunately, wasn't matched by their unquestionably humane intentions. There were others, more successful, by the great Juan Rulfo in Mexico, by the great José María Arguedas in Peru, and through them we learned of the existence of people our European culture had taught us to deny, people whose history was restricted to stories of murderous hordes, savage customs and long-lost civilizations trampled to dust under the victorious hooves of the conquistadores. The copper faces we passed every day on the street, which became more numerous the further we travelled from the capital, were invisible until, page after page, literature reminded us of their presence.

Vargas Llosa didn't follow the blood and thunder of Zola and Zola's disciples, but rather chose Flaubert as his guide. For Vargas Llosa, Flaubert (on whom he later wrote a splendid essay, *The Perpetual Orgy*) initiated the modern novel by establishing an "objective" narrator at the cost of remaining invisible, a narrator who, because he refused to preach, gave the illusion of telling a story that was true. Zola's literature seemed, to Vargas Llosa, uncomfortably close to journalism. Flaubert instead proposed the creation of a fictional reality whose facts every reader could experience and from whose fabrications every reader might learn the truth. Vargas Llosa asked, years later, in 1989:

> What is the difference between fiction and a newspaper article or a history book? Are they not all composed of words? Do they not imprison within the artificial time of the tale the boundless torrent that is real time? My answer is that they are opposing systems for approximating reality. While the novel rebels and transgresses life, those other genres can only be its slave.

Reading *The Time of the Hero* at the time of its first publication, we had no image of the author except as the eloquent, accusing narrator. He remained, as Flaubert had proposed, invisible; we felt utterly convinced that he spoke the truth, and that his fiction was staunchly objective. Throughout his following novels—*The Green House*, *Conversation in "The Cathedral"*—for which we waited with greedy expectation, the question of who this "Vargas Llosa" was kept teasing us. Then, sometime in the eighties, I gradually became conscious of his political persona. I began reading his political pronouncements about Latin America and its attendant sorrows, in which he offered suggestions to explain or mend society's ways, pronouncements that led up to his campaign for the presidency of Peru in 1990. And I was struck by the opposition between the views in his fiction and his views in the press—as if, like a sightless photographer, he were blind to the human reality that his lens had so powerfully captured.

I came to the conclusion that there are two Vargas Llosas. The first is the great novelist, the storyteller, the man so sensitive to the Other that he can recreate stories out of the Other's own experience, translating reality into fiction through a common (or commonly imagined) experience. "To create is to hold a dialogue, to write is to have always in mind the '*hypocrite lecteur, mon semblable, mon frère*' that Baudelaire speaks of. Adam and Robinson Crusoe could not have been poets, narrators," wrote this first Vargas Llosa. The second Vargas Llosa is, however, incapable of dialogue, because he is as blind as Crusoe to the Other, cannot imagine him except as a caricature of everything Vargas Llosa does not want to be. He rejects feminist and indigenist arguments because they are "politically correct," which is like rejecting "Thou shalt not kill" and "Thou shalt not steal" because they are Judeo-Christian. Like Dickens' Mr. Podsnap, this second Vargas Llosa wants to clear the world of "disagreeables" who can be swept away "with a flourish of the arm, and a flush of the face." Mr. Podsnap's "Not English!" is translated for this second Vargas Llosa into "Not white! Not Western! Not modern!"

Vargas Llosa, the novelist, defined himself and his colleagues as "professional malcontents, conscious or unconscious disturbers of society, rebels with a cause, the unredeemed revolutionaries of our world." Vargas Llosa, the politician, declared himself an anti-revolutionary, an advocate of Thatcherism, a defender of President Menem's shameful amnesty for those responsible for the disappearance of thousands of civilians during Argentina's military dictatorship, a believer in Peru's modernization, which would only be possible "with the sacrifice of Indian cultures." (As Ronald Wright observed in his response to Vargas Llosa's article in *Harper's*, where the statement appeared, "This is of course the sacrifice that many white

Peruvians have been eager to perform ever since the first of them leapt ashore with Pizarro.")

Such divided behaviour leads to a question that seems unanswerable (or even perhaps unaskable): it concerns the obligations of the writer as artist and as person. Even this dichotomy is suspect: we can read the *Odyssey* without knowing anything about Homer, but facts of time and place cling to the work like barnacles, giving an imagined shape to an author whose personal history has long vanished into dust. It is all very well to remember that a story is not necessarily the author's story, that imaginary characters don't really mouth the author's words or voice the author's opinion, that even autobiography is a form of fiction and that writers have only a fumbling idea of what it is that they've created; we want fiction to coincide with fact, and we are disturbed when Aristotle offers arguments in defence of slavery; or when the author of *Mrs. Dalloway* says to her husband, passing a plate to her in-laws at dinner, "Feed the Jews!"; or when the "unredeemed revolutionary" who roused us with *The Time of the Hero* supports an amnesty granted to torturers and argues for the annihilation of Indian cultures. We want the artist to be worthy of the art, and be the better person we ourselves would wish to be.

But *should* a work of fiction be read in the light of what we know (or think we know) about the author? Vargas Llosa himself seems to argue that it should, teasing us with parallels between his life and his work, submitting himself for scrutiny in his 1993 *A Fish in the Water*, a species of autobiography that is also a political manifesto, a memoir that reads like a curious collaboration between the two Vargas Llosas, but in which the politician Vargas Llosa seems to have had the upper hand. The book is a collection of childhood scenes, adolescent awakenings and jottings from a writer's notebook that reveal the roots of his fiction, interspersed with loud harangues by the defeated presidential candidate. It opens with an epigraph taken from Max Weber's significantly titled *Politics as a Vocation*:

> Primitive Christians also knew very explicitly that the world is ruled by demons and that anyone who becomes involved in politics, that is to say, anyone who agrees to use power and violence as a means, has sealed a pact with the devil, so that it is no longer true that in his activity the good produces only good and the bad bad, but that the contrary frequently happens.

It is tempting to read this as an accusation, the novelist quoting Weber against the politician.

When an author puts on paper, together with his other fictional characters, the fictional character that seemingly created them all, and writes, "I am the one who dreamt up these stories; I am who I tell you I am," most readers find it hard to ignore the voice calling out from the blazing bush. Vargas Llosa himself argues for the fairness of this manner of interpretation. For instance, in a clever essay on the Peruvian writer Sebastián Salazar Bondy, Vargas Llosa offers a reading of Salazar Bondy's work as merely the result of the man's social circumstances. The argument is ingenious: according to Vargas Llosa, social protest in Peru becomes for a writer the visible form of protest against his invisibility as an artist.

> Writers without publishers and without readers, with no audience to stimulate and make demands on them, or to force them to be rigorous and responsible, soon look to find the reason for this unfortunate situation. They then discover that there is blame and that this blame must be

> apportioned to certain people. The frustrated writer, reduced to solitude and the role of pariah, cannot, unless he is blind and stupid, attribute the neglect and the sorry condition of literature to men from the countryside and the suburbs who die without having learned to read and for whom, naturally, literature cannot be a vital or a superficial need because, for them, it does not exist. The writer cannot blame the lack of national culture on those who have never had the opportunity to create it because they live in conditions of constant oppression and suffocation. Their resentment, their fury, focuses logically on that privileged sector of society in Peru which knows how to read and yet does not read, on those families which have the resources to buy books and, yet do not buy them, on that class which had the means to make Peru a cultured and decent country and did not do so. (...) By the very fact of being a creator here, one belongs within the ranks of the victims of the bourgeoisie. From there, it is only one step for the writer to become conscious of this situation, take responsibility for it and declare himself a supporter of the disinherited of Peru, the enemy of their masters.

The argument is elegantly set forward, and its very elegance hides its fallacy. An appreciative audience does not necessarily lead to literary rigour and responsibility (witness the *oeuvre* of the would-be mayor of London). And to suppose that a writer will side with the disinherited merely out of spite and personal revenge is to disallow political conviction, whatever its source, and says less about the wilfulness of writers who call themselves socialists than about the murky ethics of Mario Vargas Llosa.

Following Vargas Llosa's method, then, it is fair to suggest that his political persona contributed to the astonishing failure of his 1993 novel *Death in the Andes*. Here the characters, in particular the Indian characters, are caricatures, stock figures, as lifeless as Agatha Christie's swarthy foreigners or Rider Haggard's savage Africans. In *The Time of the Hero*, the cadets came "from the jungle and the mountains, from all departments, races and economic backgrounds," and the conflict (involving murder, betrayal and revenge) stemmed not from discrimination against their class or the colour of their skin, but from the clash of individuals against the oppressive military system that demanded from them endurance of pain and blind obedience. Not any one person, but the school itself (and, on a larger scale, the whole of Peruvian society) was responsible for the tragedy. And in this, the writer once again saw clear: no single individual is at the root of evil, but rather the collective, all-encompassing social structure that determines who is in and who is out, defining itself by that which it excludes through fear and prejudice. *Death in the Andes*, on the other hand, fails not because it is a racist novel (which it is) but because its racism prevents Vargas Llosa from writing well—that is, prevents him from giving his characters, even those he abominates, a soul, as he managed to do in *The Time of the Hero*.

Vargas Llosa's hatred of the Andean Indian is evident in both his fictional and non-fictional accounts. Analysing the prejudices in which the "particolored" Peruvian society is steeped, Vargas Llosa writes in *A Fish in the Water*:

> It is a grave error, when discussing racial and social prejudices in Peru, to believe that they act only from the top down; parallel to the contempt that the white shows

> towards the mestizo, the Indian, and the black, there exists the bitterness of the mestizo against the white and the Indian and the black, and of each of these latter three against all the others, feelings—or perhaps it would be more accurate to speak of impulses or passions—that lie concealed behind political, professional, cultural, and personal rivalries, in accordance with a process which cannot even be called hypocritical, since it is rarely rational and seldom openly revealed.

As Herbert Morote has pointed out, in his essay *Vargas Llosa, Tal Cual* (San Sebastian, 1997), this is equating the hatred of the victimizer for the victim with the hatred of the victim for the victimizer. It is saying that those who for centuries have been denied their identity, their language, their culture, their most elementary rights, do wrong in showing bitterness towards their oppressors. But Vargas Llosa, the writer, knows better: "In the majority of cases, [prejudice] is unconscious, stemming from an ego that is hidden and blind to reason; it is taken in with one's mother's milk and begins to be shaped by the time of the Peruvian's first birth-cry and babblings as a baby." This doesn't, of course, justify Vargas Llosa's prejudice, but it goes some way to explain it. Interestingly enough, when Vargas Llosa writes about Indians other than those of his immediate surroundings, the faraway Amazon Indians for instance, the prejudice lifts and the novelist once again becomes articulate: these Indians are interesting, interested characters, exotic but alive, respected and respectable. This is what happens in *The Storyteller*, one of Vargas Llosa's finest achievements, a *Heart of Darkness* in which Kurtz finds at the core of the Peruvian jungle not the horror but the joy, the learning of a culture by the act of giving himself over to it, by lending it his voice in order to tell it its own stories. In Vargas Llosa's words: "Talking the way a storyteller talks means being able to feel and live in the very heart of that culture, means having penetrated its essence, reached the marrow of its history and mythology, given body to its taboos, images, ancestral desires, and terrors." The second Vargas Llosa should have this engraved in letters of fire.

In the meantime, while Vargas Llosa the politician was sealing his pact with the devil, Vargas Llosa the novelist was continuing his dialogue with the Other, and from the chronicle of the sufferings of his fellow humans he turned to the depiction of their joys. In 1988 he began writing what he himself has called "erotic fiction," and published *In Praise of the Stepmother* in the appropriately named series "The Vertical Smile," edited by Esther Tusquets in Barcelona. *The Notebooks of Don Rigoberto* followed a few years later.

Vargas Llosa once defined erotic love as a "*complicidad de fantasmas*" ("a collusion of ghosts," "a complicity of fantasies"); these ghosts or fantasies have never been absent in Vargas Llosa's work, and in *The Notebooks of Don Rigoberto* and *In Praise of the Stepmother* they have merely risen to the surface. Few contemporary erotic novels (in whatever language, I believe) explore this sensual surface without indulging in despair or pathos, few have the courage of playfulness. From Georges Bataille to Nicholson Baker, the erotic novelist normally insists on the wages of sin; Vargas Llosa instead proposes a free-for-all romp, no cover charges and no dress code enforced.

In Praise of the Stepmother is a happy version of *Phèdre* with a few minor adjustments: it is Foncho, barely an adolescent, who seduces his stepmother, the beautiful Lucrecia, while Don Rigoberto, her husband, tries to retain her through a game of ingenious erotic fantasies. Even though the novel ends badly (Lucrecia is kicked out of the house and the jealous Rigoberto is tortured by her absence), it reads like a jubilatory erotic saga, an intuition confirmed in the second volume, *The Notebooks of Don Rigoberto. In Praise of the Stepmother* proposed a series of *tableaux vivants* based on various paintings, from Jordaens's *Candaules, King of Lydia* to Fra Angelico's *Annunciation*, through which Don Rigoberto and his precocious son depict the glories of the beautiful Lucrecia. In *The Notebooks* the depictions are limited to the work of one painter, Egon Schiele, through whose tortured, vibrant, erotic paintings and drawings this Dionysian family plays out their imagined desires. Which scenes are real and which are daydreams? It doesn't matter, of course: the erotic bliss is only partly physical. Most of it is made up of words and pictures, stories and images, the lover as novelist and painter.

Vargas Llosa's language, always just this side of baroque, plays in *The Notebooks* with all manner of nuances, from the coldly descriptive to the cloyingly childish, from the mystical-amorous Spanish of the seventeenth century to the contemporary Peruvian of politics and advertising—and the translator's task is not an easy one. Compared to Spanish, English has a limited erotic vocabulary. Spanish exuberance quickly becomes in English purple prose, metaphors of sex sound arch or clinical when translated. Even the sweetest, most common nothings lack an appropriate equivalent in the reticent English tongue. And yet even with a loss of tones, Vargas Llosa's erotic tales shine through the English version, utterly joyful, a celebration of how our body imagines Paradise.

It may be that great literature, the literature that Northrop Frye defined as "possessing a vision greater in kind than that of its best readers," somehow precludes the moral ugliness of prejudice, cannot be at the same time great literature and hate literature. It may be that when a writer stoops to prejudice, he loses control over his craft and his words refuse to follow, so that he is left merely with tags and tokens, the husks of language. This happens to Neruda in his anti-Nixon poems, to Chesterton in his moments of anti-Semitic or racist bathos, to Strindberg in his diatribes against women, to Peter Handke in his excuses for the Serbian atrocities, to Pound, to Céline, to many others.

For Frye, a "major" writer is one within whose work readers can grow up "without ever being aware of a circumference." I believe this is true of the novelist Vargas Llosa, whose incommensurable books—ambitious, wise, arrogant, sprawling, intimate, pathetic, angry, playful, contradictory, illuminating—keep on relentlessly extending their boundaries well beyond the grasp of the other Vargas Llosa, their ineffectual reader.

Reading White for Black

And what shall I say of those more properly called traitors than translators, since they betray those whom they aim to reveal, tarnishing their glory, and seducing ignorant readers by reading white for black?

JOACHIM DU BELLAY,
Defense and Example of the French Tongue, 1549

We can only prohibit that which we can name.

GEORGE STEINER,
After Babel, 1973

THROUGHOUT PART OF 1992 and 1993, I worked on the translation of three short stories by the late Marguerite Yourcenar. The stories, published in French under the title *Conte Bleu*, which I rendered in English as *A Blue Tale*, are very early works by the writer who was to become, in later life, such an accomplished stylist. Understandably, since they were written with the exuberance and know-all of youth, the stories stray from time to time from sober blue to lurid purple. Since translators, unlike writers, have the possibility of amending the faults of the past, it seemed to me that to preserve every glitter and volute of Yourcenar's young text would have been nothing but a pedantic undertaking, less intended for lovers of literature than for literary urologists. Furthermore, the English language is less patient with ebullience than French. And so it was that a few times—*mea culpa, mea maxima culpa*—I silently clipped an adjective or pruned an outrageous simile.

Vladimir Nabokov, criticized by his friend Edmund Wilson for producing a translation of *Eugene Onegin* "with warts and all," responded that the translator's business was not to improve or comment on the original, but to give the reader ignorant of one language a text recomposed in *all* the equivalent words of another.[1] Nabokov apparently believed (though I find it hard to imagine that the master craftsman meant this) that languages are "equivalent" in both sense and sound, and that what is imagined in one language can be reimagined in another—without an entirely new creation taking place. But the truth is (as every translator finds out at the beginning of the first page) that the phoenix imagined in one language is nothing but a barnyard chicken in another, and to invest that singular fowl with the majesty of the bird born from its own ashes, a different language might require the presence of a different creature, plucked from bestiaries that possess their own notions of strangeness. In English, for instance, the word *phoenix* still has a wild, evocative ring; in Spanish, *ave fénix* is part of the bombastic rhetoric inherited from the seventeenth century.

In the early Middle Ages, translation (from the past participle of the Latin *transferre*, "to transfer") meant conveying the relics of a saint from one place to another. Sometimes these translations were illegal, as when the saintly remains were stolen from one town and carried away for the greater glory of another. This is how the body of St. Mark was transferred from Constantinople to Venice, hidden under a cartful of pork, which the Turkish guards at Constantinople's gates refused to touch. Carrying away something precious and making it one's own by whatever means possible: this definition serves the act of literary translation perhaps better than Nabokov's.

No translation is ever innocent. Every translation implies a reading, a choice both of subject and interpretation, a refusal or suppression of other texts, a redefinition under the terms imposed by the translator who, for the occasion, usurps the title of author. Since a translation cannot be impartial, any more than a reading can be unbiased, the act of translation carries with it a responsibility that extends far beyond the limits of the translated page, not only from language to language but often within the same language, from genre to genre, or from the shelves of one literature to those of another. In this, not all "translations" are acknowledged as such: when Charles and Mary Lamb turned Shakespeare's plays into prose tales for children, or when Virginia Woolf generously herded Constance Garnett's versions of Turgenev "into the fold of English Literature,"[2] the displacements of the text into the nursery or into the British Library were not regarded as "translations" in the etymological sense. Pork, Lamb or Woolf, every translator disguises the text with another, attractive or detractive meaning.

Were translation a simple act of pure exchange, it would offer no more possibilities for distortion and censorship (or improvement and enlightening) than photocopying or, at most, scriptorium transcription. Alas, *pace* Nabokov, it isn't. If we acknowledge that every translation, simply by transferring the text to another language, space and time, alters it for better or for worse, then we must also acknowledge that every translation—transliteration, retelling, relabelling—adds to the original text a *prêt-à-porter* reading, an implicit commentary. And that is where the censor comes in.

That a translation may hide, distort, subdue, or even suppress a text is a fact tacitly recognized by the reader who accepts it as a "version" of the original. In the index to John Boswell's ground-breaking book on homosexuality in the Middle Ages, the entry for "Translation" says "see Mistranslation"—or what Boswell calls "the deliberate falsification of historical records." The instances of asepticized translations of Greek and Roman classics are too numerous to mention and range from a change of pronoun which wilfully conceals the sexual identity of a character, to the suppression of an entire text, such as the *Amores* of the Pseudo-Lucian, which Thomas Francklin in 1781 deleted from his English translation of the author's works because it included an explicit dialogue among a group of men on whether women or boys were erotically more desirable. "But as this is a point which, at least in this nation, has been long determined in favour of the ladies, it stands in need of no further discussion," wrote the censorious Francklin.[3]

Throughout the nineteenth century, the classic Greek and Roman texts were recommended for the moral education of women only when purified in translation. The Reverend J. W. Burgon made this explicit when, in 1884, from the pulpit of New College, Oxford, he preached against allowing women into the university where they would have to study the texts in the original.

> If she is to compete successfully with men for 'honours', you must needs put the classic writers of antiquity unreservedly into her hands—in other words, must introduce her to the obscenities of Greek and Roman literature. Can you seriously intend it? Is it then a part of your programme to defile that lovely spirit with the filth of old-world civi-

> lization, and to acquaint maidens in their flower with a hundred abominable things which women of any age (and men too, if *that* were possible) would rather a thousand times be without?[4]

It is possible to censor not only a word or a line of text through translation, but also an entire culture, as has happened time and again throughout the centuries among conquered peoples. Towards the end of the sixteenth century, for instance, the Jesuits were authorized by King Philip II of Spain, champion of the Counter-Reformation, to follow in the steps of the Franciscans and establish themselves in the jungles of what is now Paraguay. From 1609 until their expulsion from the colonies in 1767, the Jesuits created settlements for the native Guaranís, walled communities called *reducciones* because the men, women and children who inhabited them were "reduced" to the dogmas of Christian civilization. The differences between conquered and conquerors were, however, not easily overcome. "What makes me a pagan in your eyes," said a Guaraní shaman to one of the missionaries, "is what prevents you from being a Christian in mine."[5] The Jesuits understood that effective conversion required reciprocity and that understanding the other was the key that would allow them to keep the pagans in what was called, borrowing from the vocabulary of Christian mystic literature, "concealed captivity." The first step to understanding the other was learning and translating their language.

A culture is defined by that which it can name; in order to censor, the invading culture must also possess the vocabulary to name those same things. Therefore, translating into the tongue of the conqueror always carries within the act the danger of assimilation or annihilation; translating into the tongue of the conquered, the danger of overpowering or undermining. These inherent conditions of translation extend to all variations of political imbalance. Guaraní (still the language spoken, albeit in a much altered form, by over a million Paraguayans) had been until the arrival of the Jesuits an oral language. It was then that the Franciscan Fray Luis de Bolaños, whom the natives called "God's wizard" because of his gift for languages, compiled the first Guaraní dictionary. His work was continued and perfected by the Jesuit Antonio Ruiz de Montoya who after several years' hard labour gave the completed volume the title of *Thesaurus of the Guaraní Tongue*. In a preface to a history of the Jesuit missions in South America,[6] the Paraguayan novelist Augusto Roa Bastos noted that, in order for the natives to believe in the faith of Christ, they needed, above all, to be able to suspend or revise their ancestral concepts of life and death. Using the Guaranís' own words, and taking advantage of certain coincidences between the Christian and Guaraní religions, the Jesuits retranslated the Guaraní myths so that they would foretell or announce the truth of Christ. The Last-Last-First-Father, Ñamandú, who created His own body and the attributes of that body from the primordial mists, became the Christian God from the Book of Genesis; Tupá, the First Parent, a minor divinity in the Guaraní pantheon, became Adam, the first man; the crossed sticks, *yvyrá yuasá*, which in the Guaraní cosmology sustain the earthly realm, became the Holy Cross. And conveniently, since Ñamandú's second act was to create the word, the Jesuits were able to infuse the Bible, translated into Guaraní, with the accepted weight of divine authority.

In translating the Guaraní language into Spanish, the Jesuits attributed to certain terms that denoted acceptable and even commendable social behaviour among the natives the connotation of that behaviour as perceived by the Catholic Church or the Spanish court. Guaraní concepts of private honour, of silent acknowledgement when accepting a gift, of a specific as opposed to a generalized knowledge, and of a social response to the mutations of the seasons and of age, were translated bluntly and conveniently as "Pride," "Ingratitude," "Ignorance" and "Instability." This vocabulary allowed the traveller Martin Dobrizhoffer of Vienna to reflect, sixteen years after the expulsion of the Jesuits, in 1783, in his *Geschichte der Abiponer*, on the corrupt nature of the Guaranís: "Their many virtues, which certainly belong to rational beings, capable of culture and learning, serve as frontispiece to very irregular compositions within the works themselves. They seem like automata in whose making have been joined elements of *pride*, *ingratitude*, *ignorance* and *instability*. From these principal sources flow the brooks of *sloth*, *drunkenness*, *insolence* and *distrust*, with many other disorders which stultify their moral quality."[7]

In spite of Jesuit claims, the new system of beliefs did not contribute to the happiness of the natives. Writing in 1769, the French explorer Louis Antoine de Bougainville described the Guaraní people in these laconic words:

> These Indians are a sad lot. Always trembling under the stick of a pedantic and stern master, they possess no property and are subjected to a laborious life whose monotony is enough to kill a man with boredom. That is why, when they die, they don't feel any regret in leaving this life.[8]

By the time of the expulsion of the Jesuits from Paraguay, the Spanish chronicler Fernández de Oviedo was able to say of those who had "civilized" the Guaraní people what a Briton,

Calgacus, is reported to have said after the Roman occupation of Britain: "The men who have perpetuated these acts call these conquered places 'peaceful.' I feel they are more than peaceful—they are destroyed."[9]

Throughout history, censorship in translation has also taken place under more subtle guises, and in our time, in certain countries, translation is one of the means by which "dangerous" authors are submitted to cleansing purges. (The Brazilian Nélida Piñón in Cuba, the decadent Oscar Wilde in Russia, Native American chroniclers in the States and Canada, the French *enfant terrible* George Bataille in Franco's Spain, have all been published in truncated versions. And, in spite of all my good intentions, could not my version of Yourcenar be considered censorious?) Often, authors whose politics might be read uncomfortably are simply not translated and authors of a difficult style are either passed over in favour of others more easily accessible or are condemned to weak or clumsy translations.

Not all translation, however, is corruption and deceit. Sometimes cultures can be rescued through translation, and translators become justified in their laborious and menial pursuits. In January 1976, the American lexicographer Robert Laughlin sank to his knees in front of the chief magistrate of the town of Zinacantán in southern Mexico and held up a book that had taken Laughlin fourteen years to compile: the great Tzotzil dictionary that rendered into English the Mayan language of 120,000 natives of Chiapas, known also as the "People of the Bat."[10] Offering the dictionary to the Tzotzil elder, Laughlin said, in the language he had so painstakingly recorded, "If any foreigner comes and says that you are stupid, asinine Indians, please show him this book, show him the 30,000 words of your knowledge, your reasoning."

It should, it must, suffice.

[1] Vladimir Nabokov, *Strong Opinions*, New York: Vintage Books, 1982.

[2] Virginia Woolf, *The Essays of Virginia Woolf, Vol. I 1912-1918*, edited by Andrew McNeillie, London: Hogarth Press, 1987.

[3] Quoted in John Boswell, *Christianity, Social Tolerance and Homosexuality: Gay People in Western Europe from the Beginning of the Christian Era to the Fourteenth Century*, Chicago & London: University of Chicago Press, 1980.

[4] Quoted in Jan Morris (ed.), *The Oxford Book of Oxford*, Oxford University Press, 1978.

[5] Quoted in *Tentación de la utopía: La República de los jesuitas en el Paraguay*, foreword by Augusto Roa Bastos, introduction and selection by Rubén Bareiro Saguier & Jean-Paul Duviols, Barcelona: Tusquets, 1991.

[6] Ibid., Bastos, Foreword.

[7] Martin Dobrizhoffer, *Geschichte der Abiponer, eine Berittenen und Kriegerischen Nation in Paraguay*, Vienna, 1783.

[8] Louis Antoine de Bougainville, *Journal du voyage autour du monde*, in *Bougainville et ses compagnons autour du monde 1766-1769*, Paris: Imprimerie Nationale, 1977.

[9] Tacitus, *Histories & Annals*, vol. 1, edited by C. H. Moore & J. Jackson, London: Loeb Classical Library, William Heinemann, 1963.

[10] Alexander Cockburn, "The Great Tzotzil Dictionary," in *Soho Square I*, edited by Isabel Fonseca, London: Bloomsbury Press, 1988.

The Secret Sharer

It is utterly impossible to persuade an Editor that he is nobody.

WILLIAM HAZLITT,
On Editors, 1819

IN 1969, TIMOTHY FINDLEY travelled to New York to work with his American editor on the galleys of his second novel, *The Butterfly Plague*. Canadian publishers were still not impressed by the efforts of this actor-turned-writer, but the illustrious American publishing company, Viking, had expressed interest in this budding author. The editor assigned to Findley's book was Corlies M. Smith, known as "Cork," who was also the editor of the letters of James Joyce. Smith read *The Butterfly Plague*, the chronicle of a declining Hollywood family set against the background of Nazi Germany, and, although he liked the book very much, wasn't satisfied with one aspect of it: he wanted to know the "meaning" of the butterflies in the story, and strongly advised Findley to make it clear. Findley was young, inexperienced, and afraid to upset the publisher he so much wanted, and bowed to Smith's suggestion. He reworked the book in order to explain the butterflies, and the novel duly appeared under the Viking imprint.

The extraordinary point of this anecdote is that most North American readers would not see it as extraordinary. Even the most inexperienced writers of fiction know that if they are to be published at all, their manuscripts must pass through the hands of professionals known as "editors," employed by publishing companies to read the books under consideration and recommend changes they think appropriate. (This paragraph you are now reading will not be the paragraph I originally wrote, since it will have to undergo the inquisition of an editor; in fact, when an earlier version of this essay was published in *Saturday Night* magazine, this sentence was cut out completely.)

Writers, notoriously wary about their craft, are reluctant to speak about this obligatory help except in general terms, or off the record. Contemporary literature abounds in examples of both malpractice and redemption, but writers prefer to keep these interventions secret—and rightly so. In the end a work of fiction is the writer's own, and should be seen as such. Writers (and their editors agree) need not make public the seams and patches of their collaboration. Writers want to be sole begetters.

However, underlying this coyness is a paradox. The writer who knows himself to be the single author of a text, wondering a little at its very existence and puzzled more than a little by the mysteries it contains, also knows that before the text is published it will be professionally questioned, and that answers will have to be provided or suggestions accepted, thereby relinquishing, in part, the writer's single-handed authorship. Before going out into the world, every writer of fiction in North America and most of the Commonwealth acquires, as it were, a literary back-seat driver.

Recognition of the profession of editor is not so ancient or widespread as the Anglo-Saxon public might suppose. In the rest of the world it is virtually unknown: even in England it appeared almost two centuries and a half after the introduction of the printing press. The Oxford English Dictionary gives

1712 as the earliest date for the mention of "editor" with the meaning "one who prepares the literary work of another," but Joseph Addison, in *The Spectator*, was using it to specify someone working on material the author had either finished or left incomplete. The "editor" understood as "one who works with the author in the fashioning of a work of fiction" didn't come into history until much later, in the first decades of the twentieth century. Before that there were only scattered references to editorial advice: Erasmus giving Thomas More suggestions regarding *Utopia*, Charles Dickens, as the editor of *Household Words*, counselling Wilkie Collins on a plot.

To find a full-fledged editor in the contemporary sense we have to wait until the 1920s, when a now legendary figure appeared in New York: Maxwell Perkins, editor of Scott Fitzgerald, Ernest Hemingway, Erskine Caldwell, and Thomas Wolfe. By all accounts, Perkins was a generous editor, keen to respect what he thought were the author's intentions—though his Samaritan urge has prevented us from knowing what Thomas Wolfe's manuscripts were like before Perkins pared them down to publishable form. With Perkins, editors acquired respectability and a patron saint. (Some might say that the patron saint of editors should be the Greek robber Procrustes, who placed his visitors on an iron bed and stretched them or cut off the overhanging parts until they fitted exactly to his liking.)

To the common reader, the precise task of an editor is something of a mystery. In a small pamphlet signed by several hands, *Author & Editor: A Working Guide* (1983), Rick Archbold, a distinguished Canadian freelance editor, attempted to elucidate: "Editors have several functions," he writes, "which vary in number according to the size and complexity of the publishing house. They may include acquiring rights to publish book projects; selling subsidiary rights; developing plans for promotion and marketing; writing copy for book jackets; ... overseeing production; and proofreading. And, of course, editing." This is not much help. Leaving aside specialized areas of publishing such as textbooks, magazines or technical non-fiction, what exactly do editors do when they say that they are "editing"?

At least one part of an editor's job, sometimes performed by a "copy editor," involves simply checking facts, spelling, grammar, compliance with the publishing company's preferred style of punctuation, etc., and asking common-sense questions: are you aware that your character is fifteen years old on page 21 and eighteen on page 34? Whatever salary an editor receives, it is probably not enough to compensate for all the thankless checking and double-checking.

Still, even this workaday aspect of editing, however necessary it may seem, has a pernicious potential. The writer who knows that his text will be inspected by an editor may see fit to leave the finer tuning unattended, because the editor will in any case try to tune the text to what sounds right to his or her own professional ear. Thomas Wolfe, submitting to Perkins's editing, would simply throw his uncorrected manuscript pages on the floor as he finished them, for the typist to collect and type out and his editor to cut and paste. Gradually the writer runs the danger of seeing himself not so much as carrying his work to where he believes he can go no farther (not finishing but abandoning his text, in Valéry's brave phrase) but as carrying his text only to the threshold of the classroom where the teacher will check spelling and grammar for him.

Copy-editing, then, is an accepted part of the editor's job. But at some point in history, probably even before the days of Maxwell Perkins, the editor bridged the chasm between questioning spelling and questioning sense, and began questioning the meaning of the butterflies. Surreptitiously, the *content* of fiction became the editor's responsibility.

In *Editors on Editing: An Inside View of What Editors Really Do* (compiled by Gerald Gross), editor, bookseller and author William Trag has this to say about what makes an editor an editor:

> A working, qualified editor of books must read. He must have read from the earliest days of his childhood. His reading must be unceasing. The *lust* for printed matter is a biological thing, a visceral and intellectual necessity; the urge must be in the genes.

In short, an editor must be a reader.

True enough. Editors must assume this function or not edit at all. But can anyone read beyond his personal inclinations? Because, to justify intrusions into an author's virgin text, an editor must surely not be Felix Chuckle who delights in happy endings or Dolores Lachrymose who prefers her endings bitter. The editor must be a sort of Platonic idea of a reader; he must embody "readerness"; he must be a Reader with a capital R.

But can even the ideal Reader help the writer? As every reader knows, literature is an act of shared responsibility. But to suppose that this mutual act allows us to know the goal the writer has set herself, a goal that in most cases is not revealed even to the writer, is either simple-minded or fatuously arrogant. To paraphrase another author, a Book is what It is. Whether the writer achieved what she intended, even knew what she intended to achieve, or in fact intended to achieve anything at all except what appears between two covers, is a mystery that no one, not even the writer, can answer truthfully.

The inappropriateness of the question comes from the richness and ambiguity that are, I believe, the true achievements of literature. "I'm not saying that it isn't in my book," said the Italian novelist Cesare Pavese in response to a critic who pointed out a metaphysical theme in his work. "I'm only saying that I didn't put it there."

When editors try to guess an author's "intention" (that rhetorical concept invented by Saint Thomas Aquinas in the thirteenth century), when they question the author about the meaning of certain passages or the reason for certain events, they are assuming that a work of literature can be reduced to a set of rules or explained in a précis. This prodding, this reductive exercise is indeed a threat, because the writer may (as Findley did) pay heed and upset the delicate balance of his creation. Older, more experienced, less afraid to alienate his publishers, Findley finally rebelled. In 1986 he revised *The Butterfly Plague*, deleting the explanation, and the new version was published by Viking Penguin.

The threat, however, is not universal. Editing understood as "a search for the author's intention" is practised almost exclusively in the Anglo-Saxon world, and less in the United Kingdom than in North America. In the rest of the world, by and large, editing means only copy-editing, a function of publishing, and even this is done with a caution that would send hundreds of editors in Chicago and Toronto in search of more challenging careers. I have worked for publishing companies in Argentina, Spain, France, Italy and Tahiti, and have visited publishing companies in Brazil, Uruguay, Japan, Germany and Sweden. Nowhere else is there such a job as our North American editors describe, and the literatures of these other countries have, to the best of my knowledge, survived very nicely.

Why is North America the hothouse of editors? I suggest that the answer lies in the mercantile fabric of American society. Because books must be saleable merchandise, experts must be employed to ensure that the products are profitably commercial. At its worst this unifying task produces mass-market romances; at its best it cuts Thomas Wolfe down to size. In Latin America, where books seldom make money, the writer is left to his own devices and a novel is welcome to stretch to whatever lengths without fear of editorial scissors.

Unfortunately, the American influence has begun to spread. In Germany and France, for instance, the *directeur de collection*, who hitherto simply chose the books she wished to publish, now sits with writers and discusses their works in progress. Sometimes the writer digs in his heels and refuses to play along. But few have either the courage or the literary clout of Graham Greene who, when his American publisher suggested changing the title of his novel *Travels with My Aunt*, replied with an eight-word telegram: "*Easier to change publisher than to change title.*"

In some cases, the writers themselves have sought this kind of professional advice, asking an editor to clarify their own intentions. The result is a peculiar collaboration. Commenting on what is perhaps the most famous case of editing in modern poetry, Ezra Pound's reworking of T. S. Eliot's *The Waste Land*, Borges remarked that "both their names should have appeared on the title page. If an author allows someone else to change his text, he is no longer the author—he is *one* of the authors, and their collaboration should be recognized as such."

Among the many lines crossed out by Pound (deletions which Eliot accepted) are these, now forever absent from the poem:

Something which we know must be dawn—
A different darkness, flowed above the clouds,
And dead ahead we saw, where sky and sea should meet,
A line, a white line, a long white line,
A wall, a barrier, towards which we drove.

The Waste Land, published after Pound's editing, has been called "the greatest poem in the English language," and yet I miss those lines and wonder whether Eliot would not have left them in, had it not been for Pound's intervention.

Of course, everywhere in the world, Anglo-Saxon or not, writers show their work before it is published (though Nabokov argued that this was like showing samples of your sputum). A gaggle of unprofessional readers—the author's mother, a neighbour, a lover, a husband or wife—performs the ritual first inspection, and offers a handful of doubts or approvals on which the author may choose or not to reflect. This contradictory chorus is not the voice of power and officialdom recommending revision.

The professional editor, on the other hand, even the most subtle and understanding, (and I have been blessed with a small number of them) tinges her opinion with the colour of authority simply because of her position. The difference between a paid editor and someone close to us is the difference between a doctor who proposes a lobotomy and a devoted aunt recommending a strong cup of tea.

The story has often been told of how Coleridge dreamt his "Kubla Khan" in an intoxication of opium, and of how, upon waking, he sat down to write it and was interrupted "by a person on business from Porlock," thereby losing forever the conclusion to that extraordinary poem. Persons from Porlock are professionally employed by the publishing companies of the Anglo-Saxon world. A few are wise and ask questions that speed on the writing; a few distract; a few quibble away at the author's vaporous confidence; a few destroy the work in mid-creation. All interfere, and it is this compulsive tinkering with someone else's text that I question.

Without editors we are likely to have rambling, incoherent, repetitive, even offensive texts, full of characters whose eyes are green one day and black the next (like *Madame Bovary*); full of historical errors, like stout Cortez discovering the Pacific (as in Keats's sonnet); full of badly strung-together episodes (as in *Don Quixote*); with a cobbled-together ending (as in *Hamlet*) or beginning (as in *The Old Curiosity Shop*). But with editors—with the constant and now unavoidable presence of editors without whose *nihil obstat* hardly a book can get published—we may perhaps be missing something fabulously new, something as incandescent as a phoenix and as unique, something impossible to describe because it has not yet been born but which, if it were, would admit no secret sharers in its creation.

VI

LOOKING TO SEE

"I don't *quite* know yet," Alice said very gently. "I should like to look around me first, if I might."

"You may look in front of you, and on both sides, if you like," said the Sheep; "but you can't look *all* round you—unless you've got eyes at the back of your head."

Through the Looking-Glass, Chapter v

The Muse in the Museum

> Museums are rubbish, a waste of time.
> Nothing should be acquired second hand.
>
> AUGUSTE RENOIR

SOMETIME IN THE MIDDLE of the first century, a man entered a museum. It was, he says, "filled with a superb collection of paintings of remarkable range and variety. There were several by Zeuxis, still untouched by the injury of time, and two or three sketches by Protogenes, so vivid and true to life that I caressed them with almost a shudder of admiration. There was also a piece by Apelles, a painting which the Greeks call the One-legged Goddess, before which I knelt with a feeling of almost religious veneration. The human figures were all executed with such striking naturalness and exquisite delicacy that it seemed as though the artist had painted their souls as well." Our visitor sees images of Zeus in the shape of an eagle taking Ganymede to Olympus; a passionate Naiad seducing the young Hylas; Apollo lamenting the death of Hyacinth. And "surrounded by these images of painted lovers," he cries out "in lonely anguish: *So even the gods in heaven are touched by love!*"

Almost two thousand years later, another man entered another museum.

> I was at the Salon d'Automne again this morning. You know how I always find the people walking about in exhibitions

so much more interesting than the paintings. This is also true of this Salon d'Automne—with the exception of the Cézanne room. There all the reality is on his side, in that thick, quilted blue of his, in his red and his shadowless green and the reddish black of his wine bottles. How humble all the objects are in his paintings. The apples are all cooking-apples and the wine bottles belong in old, round, sagging pockets. (…) And I wanted to tell you all this; *it is related to so much about us and to ourselves in a hundred places.*

The first visitor is Petronius, Petronius Arbiter, the author of that comic masterpiece, the *Satyricon*, the poet and dandy who committed suicide after denouncing the atrocities of the Emperor Nero from his deathbed.

The second visitor is Rilke, the German poet Rainer Maria Rilke, writing to his wife in 1907.

Both were writers. Both apparently frequented museums. Both found, in that which the museums had to offer, a mirror or echo of their own feelings and thoughts. Both were vastly intelligent men.

I have chosen these two examples almost at random. The relationship between writers and museums has been a long and fruitful one, and there is scarcely a writer who hasn't, at one point or another, written of what he or she has seen on a visit to a museum. In my examples, there are two formal differences: Petronius is writing a novel. The emotions he describes belong not to him but to his character, the young, cultured, lascivious Encolpius in pursuit of his ephebe, the wayward Giton. Rilke is writing a letter to his wife, the sculptor Clara Rilke. Both Petronius and Rilke, however, are trying to link that which is presented to them as art—that which is exhibited for inspection—to a private experience, to (I hope the word is not too frightening) a soul.

I find it curiously moving how little has changed and how their experiences link the German aesthete with his Roman ancestor across nineteen centuries. Both seem to be looking for the same relationship between the exhibit and the observer, and both are conducting their search within the same organized space: within a space set aside for the assembly and presentation of a group of objects under the common label of "art."

The notion that a space defines its contents was, in Petronius's time, already several centuries old. Already the Library of Alexandria, assembling not works of art but books, had established the norm and reached the same conclusion. Callimachus—the first librarian—and Petronius and Rilke, were certainly aware that catalogues contaminate that which they catalogue, infect it with meaning.

So the museum visited by Petronius's hero, and the Salon d'Automne visited by Rilke, are meaningful spaces, spaces that by their very existence lend the objects they exhibit a meaning they would otherwise not necessarily have. "Art," these spaces seem to be saying, "is what is inside a museum."

But how is the visitor affected by this knowledge? Differently, I think, in the case of Encolpius and Rilke. For Encolpius, the fame of the paintings he sees in the museum has preceded them. He observes these paintings, bringing with him the knowledge that they are important, that they have been praised by men he considers wiser than himself, and that some of them have been ennobled by tradition as great works of art. So not only are they great because of *where* they are; these paintings are great because of *what* has been said about them. Even though the Romans of the first century recognized the fallacy of the *argumentum ad auctoritatem*, the argument of authority, the perceived strength of received opinions still held fast. But this is not all Encolpius admires. Wounded by the love that has left him, he identifies in the pictures of love-anguished gods and goddesses his own torment. Beyond the picture's official fame is something else, something utterly personal, something that belongs exclusively to the paintings *only* when Encolpius is present to witness it: Encolpius's grief.

Oscar Wilde famously described art as a mirror not of life but of the spectator. The social circumstances determine, no doubt, the nature of the museum, cause it into being. But within its limits, aware or not of this frame to a greater or lesser degree, the spectator—Encolpius, in this case—is faced not with the fruit of external strictures, not with that which is shaped by the frame, but with an artistic construction that demands his private attention and to which he must respond as if he were alone in the world.

Rilke walks into his museum at a different pace. We can imagine Encolpius anxiously turning his head from image to image, searching for his reflection in the paintings that surround him, expecting a response to his lover's grief. Rilke is much more sober. The Salon d'Automne is a social gathering and, as he says, he finds "the people walking about ... so much more interesting than the paintings." In fact, for Rilke the museum institution is so evidently a social device that he takes part in it as he would any other social event. The artistic experience, the contemplation and understanding of art, cannot be, for Rilke, a collective experience. It is a miracle, but a private miracle. "But each time," he says, "the miracle is valid for the one person, only for the saints to whom it happens." This miracle takes place when he, Rilke, stands alone in a crowd in front of Cézanne's paintings. Then the revelation occurs; or perhaps, as Borges described it, what occurs is "the *imminence* of a revelation that does *not* take place." In either case, the experience is singular. It only happens to one, even if it happens a million times to a million ones.

My experience of museums has been rather varied. I have visited, like Rilke, salons in which well-dressed crowds distracted me from the paintings. I have also visited salons so empty that, as Macedonio Fernández used to say, "If one more person had been absent, he wouldn't have been able to fit." I've visited famous collections large as warehouses and small as boudoirs. I've seen exhibitions arranged as pedagogical tours and exhibitions seemingly left to the random order of chance. I've seen exhibitions where the subject prevented me from seeing the objects, and others in which the objects loudly contravened the subject. But in every case I can think of, whatever it was that was being exhibited, the experience of the museum—the salon, the gallery, the warehouse, the room, the place—was separate from that of the objects exhibited there.

My first memory of a museum is that of a Venice *palazzo*, where my nanny took me on a tour when I was five. I remember the great halls and high ceilings, and the grey-golden light that lit the dust in the rooms, and an overwhelming impression of being in a house inhabited by giant ogres. But I also remember a large painting, a battle scene, with tiny men swarming like ants on a ship in a dark-green sea, and the criss-crossing lines of the oars. And I remember that painting in vivid detail, as part of an extraordinary adventure story of which I hadn't heard the beginning and was going to miss the end. The ogres' castle was a place I visited with my nanny, and with small herds of tourists following us from room to room. The painting was my own, a battle that, from that day onwards, I saw again and again in my dreams, and to which only I had access.

Every one of our communications, every conversation, every reading, every experience of a painting or a play or a film, every contemplation of a sunset or of a remarkable face, every listening to a concert or to the song of birds, every observation answered or not, every discovery, every intuition, every revelation, every epiphany, every moment of grace, takes place somewhere defined in this world of ours by volumes of history and atlases of geography. Mozart heard at Carnegie Hall or at the entrance to a concentration camp are two different experiences, two different entities, like Heaven and Hell. The traveller who comes to either, whatever the circumstances of the journey, and however many other travellers have reached it before him, comes alone.

Society seems extraordinarily keen to state its intentions as regards its activities, as if we, social creatures, were unable to understand these activities without giving them a name. Many times, these statements are warnings (as in totalitarian societies) that the official voice will not be contravened; at other times these statements are smoke screens (as in our so-called democratic societies) meant to hide the real activities or intentions of those in power. A few, rare times, these statements are true. Museums, as social constructs, regularly undergo this labelling, and exhibitions seem constantly, even increasingly, to be under the influence of this rage for self-definition. Now I see nothing wrong with this activity, as long as we recognize it for what it is: not a true definition, only a naming. I can put together an exhibition of black art and call it "Into the Heart of Africa," thereby attempting a critical overview of the colonial missionary presence in that continent; or I can picket an exhibition of black art called "Into the Heart of Africa," thereby attempting a critical overview of the colonial missionary presence in that continent. Both activities label the exhibition;

neither determines the spectator's intimate relationship with the individual works of art therein exhibited. Obviously, the louder the label, the more difficult it will be for the spectator to abandon the social fray (as Rilke did) and stand alone, face to face with the work of art. We are made of history and geography, just as museums are, and those labels are part of that history and that geography, even if their meaning changes according to the hand pasting them on the exhibitions.

It will be said that the task of disengaging oneself from these labels is not merely difficult; it is impossible. It will be said that history and geography are not only the substance of which we are made, but that they are also that of which works of art are made. It will be said that the labels are attempts to read into the work that history and that geography.

But this hasn't been my experience. I, conditioned by time and space, change in time and space. I am constantly someone else, the person coming round the corner, the person waiting in the next room, the day after tomorrow, the person who will regret or approve what I do today, but will never repeat it. I come to a work of art with my historical and geographical baggage, but the baggage I bring is always changing and allows me to see something else in the work almost every time. Therefore I don't trust the labels. A work of art itself carries no judgement.

Of course, nothing is going to stop society from this labelling frenzy. There is a sense of security, imagined or not, in knowing that this is a modern art museum, a native craft museum, a nautical museum, a museum of natural science or black history or the Holocaust. And because we are so accustomed to these labels, even an absence of labels wouldn't save us from reading them. Imagine an exhibition of diverse works of art housed under a single roof, with no labels. One visitor will see it as official art that doesn't dare to speak its name;

another will see it as an indictment of that official art. And so on. We are beyond hope.

Or perhaps not quite. The word *museum*, the *Oxford English Dictionary* reminds us, comes from the Greek meaning "seat of the muses." Here the nine women conduct their ancient business of translating the universe into signs for us to read, each one bearing our secret name and a private warning. We may decide, as a society, decrying the notion of privilege, no longer to offer them a roof, to do away with museums. It wouldn't much matter, I think. They would assemble elsewhere, and turn the forest of Arden into their living room.

There we shall go in search of Oscar Wilde's mirrors, or, like Encolpius, to see the gods and goddesses that suffer just like ourselves, or perhaps to witness the private miracle Rilke hoped for. Bearing in mind, of course, Rilke's caveat. We may be granted the moment of grace, but we must respond to it in kind. Describing in a famous sonnet an archaic torso of Apollo, Rilke the spectator reaches this inexorable conclusion: "You must change your life."

This, I believe, is the only condition.

Dragon Eggs and Phoenix Feathers,

or A Defence of Desire

"For where no law is, there is no transgression."

Romans 4:15

I. Assembling

WE ARE TIDY CREATURES. We distrust chaos. Experiences come to us with no recognizable system, for no intelligible reason, with blind and carefree generosity. And yet, in the face of every evidence to the contrary, we believe in law and order. Anxiously, we put everything away in files, in compartments, in distinct sections; feverishly we distribute, we classify, we label. We know that this thing we call the world has no meaningful beginning or understandable end, no discernible purpose, no method in its madness. But we insist: it must make sense, it must signify something. So we divide space into regions and time into periods, and again and again we're bewildered when space refuses to hold to the reasonable limits of our atlases, and time overflows the tidy dates of our history books. We collect objects and build houses for them, in the hope that the house will give its contents coherence and a meaning. We will not accept the inherent ambiguity of any object (or collection of objects) that charms our attention, saying, like the Voice in the Burning Bush, "I am what I am." "All right," we add, "but you are also a thornbush, *Prunus spinosa*"—and give it its place on the shelf.

Of course, no object is bound to occupy exclusively any single shelf. For example: there is a story by G. K. Chesterton in which Father Brown is asked to solve the mysterious death of a Scottish lord. The only clues found in the lord's ruined castle form an odd collection. First item: a considerable hoard of precious stones without any setting whatsoever. The lord apparently kept his jewels loose in his pockets, like coins. Second item: heaps and heaps of snuff, not kept in a box or pouch but just lying on the mantelpiece or the piano. Third item: little wheels and springs of metal, as if someone had gutted a mechanical toy and left the parts scattered about. Fourth item: a number of wax candles but not a single candlestick. "By no stretch of fancy," remarks the illustrious Inspector Flambeau, "can the human mind connect together snuff and diamonds and wax and loose clockwork."

But Father Brown thinks he can see the connection. The late lord was mad against the French Revolution and tried to reenact the life of the last Bourbons. He had snuff because it was an eighteenth-century luxury; wax candles because they were the eighteenth-century lighting; bits of iron because they represented the locksmith hobby of King Louis XVI; jewels because they represented Marie-Antoinette's diamond necklace.

> "What a perfectly extraordinary notion!" cried Flambeau. "Do you really think that is the truth?"
>
> "I am perfectly sure it isn't," answered Father Brown, "only you said no one could connect snuff and diamonds

and clockwork and candles. I give you that connection off-hand. The real truth, I am very sure, lies deeper."

He then suggests that the late lord led a double life as a thief. The candles lit his way into the houses he robbed; he used snuff much as the fiercest criminals do, to throw into the eyes of his pursuers; the diamonds and cogs were used to cut his way through glass windows.

> "Is that all that makes you think it the true explanation?" asked the Inspector.
>
> "I don't think it the true explanation," replied the priest placidly; "but you said that nobody could connect the four things."

It might be something simpler, says Father Brown. The late lord found diamonds on his estate and kept the find a secret. The wheels were used to cut the stones. Snuff was used to bribe the Scottish peasants into searching the caves by the light of the candles.

> "Is that all?" asked Flambeau after a long pause. "Have we got to the dull truth at last?"
>
> "Oh no," said Father Brown.... "I only suggested that because you said one could not plausibly connect snuff with clockwork or candles with bright stones. Ten false philosophies will fit the universe."

And a thousand false systems will invent an order for our world.

The curious construction known as a museum is, above all, a place of order, of organized space, of predetermined sequences. Even a museum that houses an apparently heterogeneous collection of objects, assembled, it would seem, without a clear purpose, becomes defined (as I've said previously) by a label outside the particular identity of each of its pieces: the identity of their collector, for instance. The first university museum—the first museum built for the purpose of studying a specific group of objects—was the Ashmolean Museum in Oxford, founded in 1683. At its core was a collection of strange and wonderful things amassed by two John Tradescants, father and son, in the previous century, and sent to Oxford by barge from London. These treasures included:

> A Babylonian Vest.
> Diverse sorts of Egges from Turkie; one given for a Dragons egge.
> Easter Egges of the Patriarchs of Jerusalem.
> Two feathers of the Phoenix tayle.
> The claw of the bird Rock: who, as Authors report, is able to trusse an Elephant.
> Dodar, from the island Mauritius; it is not able to flie being so big.
> Hares head, with rough horns three inches long.
> Toad fish, and one with prickles.
> Divers things cut on Plum-stones.
> A Brazen-balle to warme the Nunnes hands.

Like snuff and candles, diamonds and clockwork, a Phoenix's feather and a nun's warming-ball have little in common. However, what holds that extraordinary list together is the fascination these objects produced, three centuries ago, in the minds and hearts of the two John Tradescants. Whether these objects represented the Tradescants' greed or curiosity, their vision of the world or a reflection of the dark map of their souls, those who visited the Ashmolean in the late seventeenth-century would enter a space ordered, so to speak, by the Tradescants' ruling passion.

I have said that we are tidy creatures, that we seek order. We know, however, that no order is innocent, not even the order of a private passion. Any categorical system imposed on objects or people or ideas must be suspect since, of necessity, it contaminates with meaning those very ideas, people, objects. The candles and clockwork of Father Brown's story are tinged with the quality of his ironical ordering; the Babylonian vest and the Easter eggs of the Ashmolean formulate a seventeenth-century idea of private property.

A brief chronology of a few such ordering forces might be of some use here.

The habit of exposing one's private passions to the public view can be traced, in Europe, to the late fifteenth century. At a time when heads of state had begun to amass some of the world's greatest collections or art—in Vienna, the Vatican, in Spain's El Escorial, in Florence and Versailles—smaller, more personal collections were also being formed. One such collection is that of Isabella d'Este, wife of the Marquis of Mantua, who, rather than purchasing art for religious reasons or to furnish a house, began collecting works of art for the sake of the works of art themselves. Up to then, the wealthy collected art mainly to lend a space beauty or prestige. Isabella set aside a space that would instead lend a frame to certain collected works of art. In her *camerino*—a "room" that was to become famous in the history of art as one of the earliest private museums—Isabella exhibited "paintings with a story" by the best contemporary artists. She had a good eye: she instructed her agent to approach Mantegna, Giovanni Bellini, Leonardo,

Perugino, Giorgione, Raphael and Michelangelo for their work. Several of them complied.

A century later, the collecting passion took over the homes not only of the aristocratic rich but also of the bourgeoisie, and the governing order of such collections was largely one of social status, whether monetary or scholarly. What Bacon called "a model of the universal nature made private" could be seen in the parlours of many lawyers and physicians. Sometimes, when cash was lacking, these collectors resorted to ingenious devices. In 1620, the scholar Cassiano dal Pozzo assembled, in his house in Rome, not the original works of art, the authentic models of famous buildings, the natural history specimens sought after by his wealthier peers, but drawings, commissioned from professional draughtsmen, of all kinds of strange objects, creatures and antiquities. He called this his "Paper Museum." Here again, as in Isabella's *camerino* and in the Tradescants' collection, the ruling design, the imposed order, was personal, a *gestalt* created by a private history—with one added characteristic: the objects themselves were no longer required to be "the real thing." These could now be replaced by their representations, their imaginings. And since these "reproductions" were much cheaper and easier to come by than the originals, the "Paper Museum" suggested that not only the very wealthy could become collectors—the owners, so to speak, of the spoils of history.

In France, at least until the French Revolution, the accepted truth had been that history was the prerogative of a single class. When in 1792, in the tide of social change, the Louvre Palace was turned into a museum for the people, the novelist Viscount François-René de Chateaubriand, voicing a haughty complaint against the notion of a common past, protested that works of art thus assembled "had no longer anything to say either to the imagination or the heart." When, a few years later, the artist and antiquarian Alexandre Lenoir founded a Museum of French Monuments to preserve the statuary and masonry of the mansions, monasteries, palaces and churches that the Revolution had plundered, Chateaubriand dismissively described it as "a collection of ruins and tombs from every century, assembled without rhyme nor reason in the cloisters of the Petits-Augustins."

In both the official and the private world of collectors, Chateaubriand's criticism went staunchly unheard. After the Revolution, the collecting of ancient things stopped being an exclusively aristocratic entertainment and became a bourgeois hobby, first under Napoleon and his love for the trappings of Ancient Rome, and later under the Republic. By the beginning of the nineteenth century, the displaying of fusty bric-à-brac, old masters' paintings and ancient books had become a fashionable pastime of the middle classes. Curiosity shops flourished. Antique dealers amassed caches of prerevolutionary treasures, which were bought and then displayed in the home museums of the *nouveaux riches*. In these nineteenth-century bourgeois homes, art and beauty denoted leisure; usefulness was left to the workers. "Living?" asked the aristocratic Villiers de L'Isle Adam. "The servants will do that for us!" In such a spirit, the museum became a utopian space, the explicit embodiment of a class philosophy.

The next remarkable change took place in the first half of our century, when the museum became a marketplace. Throughout the world, but especially in North America where collections turned into symbols of public status, museums multiplied like mushrooms. These new museums were required to respond to three distinct and growing fears, which the new collectors, working within the confines of a mercantile society and under the shadow of the two world wars, were experiencing: fear of loss, fear of deterioration and fear of excess. The first required a building that would not scatter a collection, since value was seen as cumulative. The second required precautions that would protect the collection from the ruin of time and from theft. The third demanded that the space allow for the collection's growth—for storage and rotation. And since the competition was fierce, codes beyond the aesthetic code were established to determine what was a work of art and what was an artefact, what was prestigious and therefore valuable, and what was nothing more than a quirky roadshow attraction. Suddenly, the museum itself took on the role of critic and the mere act of exhibiting something in a museum defined its nature. The museum now claimed to offer a "real" presentation of the object displayed: that is to say, the object in its three dimensions (even as a reproduction, as in the "Paper Museum") but not as a description or gloss. This reality was, of course, not tangible but accepted as an act of faith. The "hands off" rule placed the object literally on a pedestal, elevating it to the category of precious specimen, granting it a kind of aristocracy through the very act of enthroning it.

The arbitrary essence of this process was something Marcel Duchamp recognized very clearly when as early as 1914 he exhibited a bicycle wheel under the title "Bicycle Wheel." According to Duchamp, the label and the space in which the object was exhibited ironically bestowed upon the object a higher status. With this one act, Duchamp appropriated the museum's role as critic in defining the work of art, and incorporated criticism into the creation itself.

II. Taking Apart

But all these orders, all these systems, all these methods of grouping and arranging objects within a given space, all these different grammars that structure the elements of a collection in a certain sequence and with a certain meaning, required their counterpart, their mirror, their recipient—their reader. With the creation of the public museums, a new invention, the public, was willed into existence. And with it arose the problem of access.

When a private, personal, secret collection becomes public, or when a certain authority decides to open the doors to a public museum, the individual pieces of the collection momentarily lose their singular identity as works of art or archeological remains, as natural history specimens or examples of any one human activity, and form together an assembly larger than (and different from) its individual parts. Together, they become the *definition* of a specific category or concept: "Modern Art" or "Prehistoric Culture," "The Craft of Coffee-Making" or "Military History," "The Life of Dickens" or "Jewish Tradition." Within the borders of the Winnipeg Art Gallery, a Joyce Wieland painting is not what it was coming from the artist's hands, or what it might have become in Conrad Black's living-room, but, for instance, an example of twentieth-century Canadian art. Within the confines of the Calgary Glenbow Museum a Blackfoot blanket is not something beautiful woven to keep someone warm, but a trace of a codified native past (for some) or an accusation of imperialist appropriation (for others). Space defines what it contains in both specific and general terms, with one embracing label for all—a label meant to be "democratically" perceived by that other collective invention, the public.

And yet, when this public gains access to the diverse objects that have become amalgamated under one roof, a paradox arises. In order for the public to perceive the collection beyond the all-encompassing label of the museum's name, it must *dis-associate* each piece from the whole, it must see it out of context, it must restore to it its individuality. This is especially true in the case of works of art; in order to "read" an object, the viewers must turn away from the explicative labels, dismiss the helpful historical and geographical notes provided by the curator, forget the criticisms, the catalogue copy, the reviews, and stand in front of the work of art ready to *not understand* everything, in that half-comprehension of an æsthetic or emotional reaction, recreating, as far as possible, the mystery of creation.

To do this, one further paradoxical step is required. The arduously invented "public," the people to whom the populist movements, such as the French Revolution, strove to give access to art, the flocking crowd which every government requires in order to justify its existence, must in turn be dissolved. Groups, guides and organized tours that lead an audience through a museum's maze are all very well—superficially. Their activity is part of sightseeing, not of looking; of cultural propaganda, not of learning; of communal bonding to the conventions of a class or an age, seldom an epiphany. To see, the public must become single again, recognize and confront the official views; the viewer must be alone in front of a lonely creation, and name for himself or herself whatever happens to touch the soul. The whole notion on which the idea of museum is based—a collective display for a collective audience—must be undermined, dispelled, destroyed, for the experience of visiting a museum to have sense beyond mere tourism. For a museum to be a place of revelation, the idea of museum itself must be contested.

Access, therefore, must be individual in order to be effective. In Europe, for instance, it is not a question of more access but of less or better planned access. The most prestigious museums can barely cope with the floods of visitors and long impatient queues. The act of visiting a museum has become akin to that of a bureaucratic transaction: waiting in line, being shuffled around, being told what to do and what to admire, following an official code that dictates what is important so that the visitor's passport can bear the stamp "I came, I saw, I conquered." These days it takes strategies (just like the ones used to circumvent official red tape) to be able to spend some time actually *looking* at the paintings in exhibitions such as the Cézanne retrospective at the Paris Grand Palais or the Goya at the Prado in Madrid: finding out the hours of least affluence, booking ahead when tickets are pre-sold, avoiding guided groups and the horrible buzzing of leaking audioguides. It is obvious that in these cases longer hours are needed, or controlled visiting times—which means a further stretching of the museum's limited budget.

At the Louvre, where attendance has increased dramatically in the past few years, the administration has found ingenious ways of dealing with the problem of crowds. Even though the waiting is still long at certain hours, once you descend into the well-lit bowels of the museum under the glass pyramid, you stand like Dorothy at the crossroads of Oz, faced with several tempting choices, and it is possible to plan a fairly uncrowded itinerary: the new disposition of the museum allows this. Furthermore, the special exhibitions encourage visits by those who have already accomplished the traditional circuit. Selecting one painting, for instance, and creating an exhibition around it, allows the viewer a detached concentration and the possibility of understanding the painting's context. Another effective idea at the Louvre is to offer the rich reserves (mainly from the drawings and engravings department, less visited) to a non-professional curator—the critic Jean Starobinski or the film-maker Peter Greenaway—to choose a subject and create an exhibition around it. These exhibitions were very successful and divert the flow of visitors from other sections of the museum.

Museums, then, should perhaps encourage, through an unfamiliar architecture, their own disregard. The huge, palatial, awe-inspiring structures of the nineteenth century that said to their visitors "You are about to enter a temple, a place greater than any of your homes" were, in spite of their autocratic intentions, right in this: in providing an unfriendly, even forbidding ground, they made it possible for the viewer not to take the view for granted, to recognize that the assumption of importance was indeed assumed, and that the voice of authority had, in its marble and gilded frames, superseded the voice of experience. The obviousness of the Louvre's authoritarian architecture led Duchamp to say in his old age that he hadn't stepped inside the Louvre for over twenty years because its collection was arbitrary and arbitrary also the value attributed to it; that all sorts of other paintings could replace those that hung on its venerable walls and that he didn't want to lend validity to the official choice with his presence.

However, for those visitors who can differentiate between the container and its contents, between the collection and the individual paintings collected, between the uniforming space and the uniformed desire, a visit to the Louvre can be a private and self-defining journey, and the relationship of a particular visitor to a particular painting may be that of Robinson Crusoe and the lonely island that he must suffer and yet inhabit—with all its mysteries, its dangers, its difficulties, its never-exhausted marvels.

In her novel *Beloved*, Toni Morrison writes: "To get to a place where you could love anything you chose—not to need permission for desire—well now, *that* was freedom." Museums can be such a place, and yet cannot exist without a structure, without an ordered display. Because it is in the nature of any exhibit that its formation, willed or not, explicit or not, allows us who come to it, the public, to read in it a pre-established order, to see a "tidied-up" version of the original material so that our itinerary through it appears intelligible. But at the same time, to experience the freedom necessary to go beyond the labelled reading of any work or art, to recover the aesthetic experience that always and necessarily lies on the verge of consciousness, we need to disrupt that perceived order, confront it, question it. To break rules we need rules, and those a museum will provide. The somewhat forbidding quality of a museum's space, the implied hierarchies in a museum's display, and the varying degrees of difficulty with which access is gained to a museum's collections are essential parts of a fruitful aesthetic experience. It is not the museum but the public that must be accessible to wonder; each visitor must claim for himself a dragon's egg or a feather of the phoenix. And the public must make itself accessible, not as a uniform and idealized mass, but as a heterogeneous collection of individuals, bringing specific desires and varying concepts of healthy anarchy into the labelled halls of a museum. Because as we all know, desire is not a collective force, but something essentially intimate, a private sense with which to explore the world, akin to taste or to hearing.

On the 1937 façade of the Musée de l'Homme in Paris are carved the following words, by Paul Valéry, giving the *mot de passe* for anyone standing at the museum's doors, demanding access.

It depends on those who enter
That I become tomb or treasure
That I speak or remain silent.
You alone must decide.
Friend, enter not unless filled with desire.

VII

CRIME AND PUNISHMENT

"There's the King's Messenger. He's in prison now, being punished: and the trial doesn't even begin till next Wednesday: and of course the crime comes last of all."

"Suppose he never commits the crime?" said Alice.

"That would be all the better, wouldn't it?" the Queen said.

Through the Looking-Glass, Chapter v

In Memoriam

"I went to the Classical master, though. He was an old crab, *he* was."

"I never went to him," the Mock Turtle said with a sigh. "He taught Laughing and Grief, they used to say."

"So he did, so he did," said the Gryphon, sighing in his turn; and both creatures hid their faces in their paws.

Alice's Adventures in Wonderland, Chapter IX

WHERE TO BEGIN?

Every Sunday from 1963 to 1967, I had lunch not at my parents' home but in the house of the novelist Marta Lynch. She was the mother of one of my schoolmates, Enrique, and she lived in a residential suburb of Buenos Aires, in a big villa with a red-tiled roof and a flower garden. Enrique had discovered that I wanted to be a writer, and offered to show his mother some of my stories. I agreed. A week later Enrique handed me a letter. I remember the blue paper, the wobbly typing, the big, ungainly signature, but most of all I remember the overwhelming generosity of those few pages and the warning at the end: "My son," she wrote, "congratulations. And I pity you more than you can know." Only one other person, a Spanish teacher at school, had told me that literature could be so important. Together with the letter was an invitation to lunch on the following Sunday. I was fifteen.

I hadn't read Marta's first novel, a semi-autobiographical account of her political and amorous involvement with one of the few civilian presidents who came to power after Perón's ousting. It had won an important literary prize and procured for her the kind of fame that made journalists ring her up for opinions on the Vietnam War and the length of summer skirts, and her large, sensuous face, made dreamy by big eyes that seemed always half closed, appeared every other day in a magazine or a newspaper.

So every Sunday, before lunch, Marta and I sat on a large flowered couch and, in an asthmatic voice that I thought breathless with excitement, she talked about books. After lunch, Enrique, I and a few others—Ricky, Estela, Tulio—would sit around a table in the attic and discuss politics, the Rolling Stones complaining in the background. Ricky was my best friend, but Enrique was the one we envied because he had a steady girlfriend, Estela, who was then twelve or thirteen, and whom he eventually married.

I have found that in Canada the idea of a group of teenagers earnestly discussing politics is almost inconceivable. But to us, politics were part of everyday life. In 1955 my father had been arrested by the military government that had overthrown Perón, and as coup followed government coup we grew accustomed to the sight of tanks rolling down the street as we walked to school. Presidents came and went, school principals would be replaced according to party interests, and by the time we reached high school the vagaries of politics had taught us that the subject called "Civic Education"—a obligatory course taught in school on the democratic system—was an amusing fiction.

The high school Enrique and I attended was the Colegio Nacional de Buenos Aires. The year we entered, 1961, a genius in the ministry of education had decided that a pilot scheme would be tested here. The courses, instead of being taught by ordinary high-school teachers, would be in the hands of university professors, many of whom were writers, novelists, poets as well as critics and arts journalists. These teachers had the right (were in fact encouraged) to teach us very specialized aspects of their subject. This didn't mean that we were allowed to overlook generalities; it meant that, besides acquiring an overview of, say, Spanish literature, we would spend a whole year studying in great detail a single book, *La Celestina* or *Don Quixote*. We were extremely lucky: we were given essential information and we were taught how to think about particulars, a method we could later apply to the world at large and to our own agonizing country in particular. Discussing politics was unavoidable. None of us thought that our studies stopped at the end of a textbook.

I've mentioned that prior to Marta Lynch's encouragement, one other person had told me that literature was a serious activity. Our parents had explained to us that artistic endeavours were not truly valid occupations. Sports were good for the body, and a little reading, like Brasso, gave one a nice shine, but the real subjects were mathematics, physics, chemistry, and at a pinch history and geography. Spanish was lumped together with music and the visual arts. Because I loved books (which I collected with miserly passion) I felt the guilty shame of someone in love with a freak. Ricky, who accepted my quirk with the magnanimity of a true friend, always gave me books for my birthday. Then, on the first day of our second year of high school, a new teacher walked into the classroom.

I will call him Rivadavia. He walked in, barely said good afternoon, didn't tell us what the course would be or what his expectations were, and opening a book, began to read something which began like this: "Before the door stands a doorkeeper on guard. To this doorkeeper there comes a man from the country who begs admittance to the Law. But the doorkeeper says that he cannot admit the man at that moment ..." We had never heard of Kafka, we knew nothing of parables, but that afternoon the floodgates of literature were opened for us. This was nothing like the dreary bits of classics we had had to study in our grade five and six readers; this was mysterious and rich, and it touched on things so personal that we would never have acknowledged they concerned us. Rivadavia read us Kafka, Cortázar, Rimbaud, Quevedo, Akutagawa; mentioned what the new critics were reviewing and quoted from Walter Benjamin and Merleau-Ponty and Maurice Blanchot; encouraged us to see *Tom Jones* even though it was rated R; told us about having heard Lorca recite his own poems one day in Buenos Aires "in a voice full of pomegranates." But above all, he taught us how to read. I don't know if all of us learned, probably not, but listening to Rivadavia guide us through a text, through the relationships between words and memories, ideas and experiences, encouraged me towards a lifetime of addiction to the printed page from which I have never managed to wean myself. The way I thought, the way I felt, the person I was in the world, and that other, darker person I was all alone by myself, were for the most part born on that first afternoon in which Rivadavia read to my class.

Then, on June 28, 1966, an army coup led by General Juan Carlos Onganía overturned the civil government. Troops and tanks surrounded the government palace, only a few blocks away from our school, and President Arturo Illia, old and frail (cartoonists portrayed him as a tortoise) was kicked out into the streets. Enrique insisted that we organize a protest. Dozens of us stood on the steps of the school chanting slogans, refusing to go to class. A few of the teachers joined the strike. There were scuffles. One of our friends got his nose broken in a fight with a pro-military group.

In the meantime, the meetings at Enrique's house continued. Sometimes we were joined by Estela's younger brother, sometimes only Enrique and Ricky attended. I became less interested. On a few Sundays I left after lunch with some uneasy excuse. Marta Lynch published several more novels. She was now one of the best-selling authors in Argentina (which did not mean that she was making any money) and she longed for some success abroad, in the United States, in France. It never happened.

After graduation, I spent a few months at the University of Buenos Aires studying literature, but the plodding pace and the unimaginative lectures made me sick with boredom. I suspect that Rivadavia and the critics he had introduced us to had spoilt my enjoyment of a straightforward course: after being told, in Rivadavia's thundering voice, of Ulysses' adventures through a Borges story, "The Immortal," in which the narrator is Homer, alive throughout the ages, it was difficult to listen for hours to someone drone on about the textual problems in early transcriptions of the *Odyssey*. I left for Europe on an Italian ship in the early months of 1968.

For the next fourteen years Argentina was flayed alive. Anyone living in Argentina during those years had two choices: either to fight against the military dictatorship or allow it to flourish. My choice was that of a coward: I decided not to return. My excuse (there are no excuses) is that I would not have been good with a gun. During my European peregrinations I kept hearing, of course, about the friends I'd left behind.

My school had always been known for its political activities, and throughout history many notable Argentinian politicians had come from the same classrooms in which I had sat. Now it seemed as if the government had specifically targeted not only the school but my schoolmates. News about them began to trickle out, month after month. Two friends (one had taught himself to play the oboe and gave impromptu performances in his room; the other had observed that those performances were "more boring than dancing with your own sister") were shot dead at a petrol station just outside Buenos Aires. Another friend, whose name now seems to have vanished with her, so small she seemed to be about twelve when I last saw her, aged sixteen, was caught in a raid, chained to other prisoners by the feet, and dropped from a military plane into the Rio de la Plata. Estela's brother, barely fifteen, disappeared one afternoon on his way to the movies. His corpse was delivered, inside a mail bag, to his parents' doorstep, so badly mangled it was hardly recognizable. Enrique left for Spain. Ricky escaped to Brazil. Marta Lynch committed suicide. She shot herself in the kitchen while outside a taxi was waiting to take her to an interview at a radio station. The note she left read simply, "I can bear all this no longer."

A few years ago I found myself in Brazil on a stopover. Back in Buenos Aires, one of my brothers had run into Ricky's mother and she had given him Ricky's address in Rio, which my brother then forwarded to me. I called him. He was now married, with kids, teaching economics at the university. I kept trying to understand what had changed in him because he didn't look older, merely different. I realized that everything he did now seemed slowed down—his speech, his gestures, the way he moved. A certain flabbiness had overtaken him; little seemed to excite him.

He had made a home in Brazil now—his wife, his children were Brazilian, but it was still a foreign country. He told me that in exile, as he called it, he had become part of a "memory group." Memory groups, he explained, were in charge of recording political crimes so that nothing might be forgotten. They had lists of names of torturers, spies, informants. The Commission on the "Desaparecidos" in Argentina, set up by President Alfonsín in 1983 to investigate the fate of the thousands who disappeared during the military dictatorship, later recorded the testimony of the surviving victims. The memory groups kept records of the victimizers, in the hope that one day they would be brought to justice. I suspect that some of Ricky's despondency came from the fact that he foresaw the outcome of the trials Alfonsín had promised: a few sentences, a few reprimands, and then the general amnesty proclaimed in 1991 by the new president, Carlos Menem.

I mentioned how extraordinary it seemed that our friends, our school, had been a target of the government. Ricky said that the military had depended on informants. That inside the school there were those who provided the torturers with details about our activities, with names, addresses, character descriptions. I agreed that there were those who had always publicly supported the military, but that there was a fair distance between waving a pro-military banner and actually collaborating with torturers.

Ricky laughed and said that I obviously had no idea of how those things worked. The military hadn't depended on a group of kids chanting things like "Homeland, Family, Church." They needed intelligent, resourceful people. Such as Rivadavia. Ricky said his group had solid proof that for several years Professor Rivadavia had passed on to the military government detailed information about us—his students. Not simply the names, but careful notes on our likes and dislikes, on our family backgrounds and school activities. He knew us all so well.

Ricky told me this a few years ago, and I have never stopped thinking about it. I know Ricky wasn't mistaken. In my mind, I have three options:

- I can decide that the person who was of the uttermost importance in my life, who in a way allowed me to be who I am now, who was the very essence of the illuminating and inspiring teacher, was in fact a monster and that everything he taught me, everything he had encouraged me to love, was corrupt.
- I can try to justify his unjustifiable actions and ignore the fact that they led to the torture and death of my friends.
- I can accept that Rivadavia was both the good teacher *and* the collaborator of torturers, and allow that description to stand, like water and fire.

I don't know which of these options is the right one.

Before saying goodbye, I asked Ricky if he knew what had become of Rivadavia. Ricky nodded and said that Rivadavia had left the school and entered a small publishing company in Buenos Aires, and that he wrote book reviews for one of the major Argentinian newspapers.

As far as I know, he is still there.

God's Spies

There is a remedy in human nature against
tyranny, that will keep us safe under every form
of government

SAMUEL JOHNSON

... And take upon's the mystery of things
As if we were God's spies; and we'll wear out
In a walled prison, packs and sects of great ones
That ebb and flow by th' moon.

King Lear, V:2

OUR HISTORY IS THE STORY of a long night of injustice: Hitler's Germany, Stalin's Russia, the South Africa of apartheid, Ceauşescu's Romania, the China of Tiananmen Square, McCarthy's America, Castro's Cuba, Pinochet's Chile, Stroessner's Paraguay, endless others form the map of our time. We seem to live either within or just on this side of despotic societies. We are never secure, even in our small democracies. When we think of how little it took for upright French citizens to jeer at convoys of Jewish children being herded into trucks, or for educated Canadians to throw stones at women and old men in Oka, we have no right to feel safe.

The trappings with which we rig our society so that it will remain a society must be solid, but they must also be flexible. That which we exclude and outlaw or condemn must also remain visible, must always be in front of our eyes so that we can live by making the daily choice of not breaking these social bonds. The horrors of dictatorship are not inhuman horrors: they are profoundly human—and therein lies their power. Any system of government based on arbitrary laws, extortion, torture, slavery lies at a mere hand's-grasp from our own democratic systems.

Chile has a curious motto, "By Reason or by Force." It can be read in at least two ways: as a bully's threat, with an accent on the second part of the equation, or as an honest recognition of the precariousness of any social system, adrift (as the Mexican poet Amado Nervo said) "between the clashing seas of force and reason." We, in most Western societies, believe we have chosen reason over force, and for the time being we can depend on that conviction. But we are never entirely free from the temptation of power. At best, our society will survive by upholding a few common notions of humanity and justice, dangerously sailing, as my own Canadian motto has it, *A mari usque ad mare*, between those two symbolic seas.

Auden famously declared that "Poetry makes nothing happen." I don't believe that to be true. Not every book is an epiphany, but many times we have sailed guided by a luminous page or a beacon of verse. What role poets and storytellers have on our precarious journeys may not be immediately clear, but perhaps some form of an answer emerged in the aftermath of one particular dictatorship, one that I followed closely over the bloody decade of its rule.

I can't remember her name but she was one grade below mine at the Colegio Nacional de Buenos Aires. I met her in my second year of high school, on one of the excursions our zealous supervisors liked to organize for us, during which we discovered the art of rigging up tents, a taste for reading Rulfo and Hemingway around the campfire, and the mystery of politics. What exactly these politics were we never quite found out, except that at the time they echoed, somewhat bombastically, our vague notions of freedom and equality. In time, we read (or tried to read) arid books on economy and sociology and history, but for most of us politics remained a serviceable word that named our need for comradeship and our contempt for authority. The latter included the school's conservative headmaster; the remote landowners of vast areas of Patagonia (where, at the foot of the Andes, we went camping and where, as I have mentioned, we saw peasant families living out their distant and for us inconceivable lives); and the military, whose tanks, on 28 June 1966, we saw lumber through the streets of Buenos Aires, one of many such processions towards the presidential palace on Plaza de Mayo. She was sixteen that year; in 1968 I left Buenos Aires and never saw her again. She was small, I remember, with black and curly hair which she had cut very short. Her voice was unemphatic, soft and clear, and I could always recognize her on the phone after just one syllable. She painted, but without much conviction. She was good at maths. In 1982, shortly before the Malvinas War and towards the end of the military dictatorship, I returned to Buenos Aires for a brief visit. Asking for news of old friends, so many dead and disappeared in those terrible years, I was told that she was among the missing. She had been kidnapped leaving the university where she had sat on the student council. Officially, there was no record of her detention, but someone had apparently seen her at El Campito, one of the military concentration camps, in a brief moment when her hood had been removed for a medical inspection. The military usually kept their prisoners hooded so that they would not be able to recognize their torturers.

On 24 April 1995, Victor Armando Ibañez, an Argentinian sergeant who had served as a guard at El Campito, gave an interview to the Buenos Aires newspaper *La Prensa*. According to Ibañez, between 2,000 and 2,300 of those imprisoned there, men and women, old people and adolescents, were "executed" by the army at El Campito during the two years of his service, from 1976 to 1978. When the prisoners' time came, Ibañez told the newspaper, "they were injected with a strong drug called pananoval, which made a real mess of them in a few seconds. It produced something like a heart attack. [The injections would leave the prisoners alive but unconscious.] Then they were thrown into the sea. We flew at a very low altitude. They were phantom flights, without registration. Sometimes I could see very large fish, like sharks, following the plane. The pilots said that they were fattened by human flesh. I leave the rest to your imagination," Ibañez said. "Imagine the worst."[1]

Ibañez's was the second "official" confession. A month earlier, a retired navy lieutenant commander, Adolfo Francisco Scilingo, had confessed to the same method of "disposing of the prisoners." In response to his confession, Argentinian President Carlos Menem called Scilingo a "criminal," reminded the press that the commander had been involved in a shady automobile deal and asked how could the word of a thief be counted as true. He also ordered the navy to strip Scilingo of his rank.

Since his election in 1989, Menem had been trying to shelve the whole question of military culpability during the so-called "dirty war" that ravaged Argentina from 1973 to 1982, and during which over thirty thousand people were killed.[2] Not content with the deadline for filing charges against the military (which his predecessor, Raúl Alfonsín had set as 22 February

1988), on 6 October 1989 Menem had offered most of the military involved in human rights abuses a general pardon. A year later, three days after Christmas, Menem issued a general amnesty to all involved in the events that had bled the country for nine long years. Accordingly, he released from prison Lieutenant General Jorge Videla (who was later re-arrested) and General Roberto Viola, both of whom had been appointed to the presidency by the military junta, from 1976 to 1981 and for ten months in 1981 respectively. In legal terms, a pardon implies not an exoneration or acquittal but only a relief from punishment. An amnesty on the other hand (such as the military had granted itself *in extremis* in 1982, and which was repealed by Alfonsín) is, in effect and intention, a recognition of innocence that wipes away any imputation of crime. After the declarations of Scilingo and Ibañez, President Menem briefly threatened the military with a retraction of the 1990 amnesty.

Until the confessions of 1995, the Argentinian military had recognized no wrongdoing in their so-called anti-terrorist activities. The extraordinary nature of guerrilla war demanded, the military said, extraordinary measures. In this declaration they were well advised. In 1977, following a joint report from Amnesty International and the American State Department's human rights bureau accusing the Argentinian security forces of being responsible for hundreds of disappearances, the military hired an American public relations company, Burson-Marsteller, to plan its response. The 35-page memorandum presented by Burson-Marsteller recommended that the military "use the best professional communications skills to transmit those aspects of Argentine events showing that the terrorist problem is being handled in a firm and just manner, with equal justice for all."[3] A tall order, but not impossible in the age of communication. As if moved by the hackneyed motto "The pen is mightier than the sword," Burson-Marsteller suggested that the military appeal for "the generation of positive editorial comment" from writers "of conservative or moderate persuasions." As a result of their campaign, the ex-governor of California, Ronald Reagan, declared in the *Miami News* of 20 October 1978 that the State Department's human rights office was "making a mess of our relations with the planet's seventh largest country, Argentina, a nation with which we should be close friends."

Over the years, others answered the advertisers' appeal. In 1995, shortly after Ibañez's and Scilingo's confessions, an article appeared in the Spanish newspaper *El País*, signed by Mario Vargas Llosa. Under the title "Playing with Fire," Vargas Llosa argued that, horrible though the revelations might be, they were not news to anyone, merely confirmations of a truth "atrocious and nauseating for any half-moral conscience." "It would certainly be wonderful," he wrote, "if all those responsible for these unbelievable cruelties were taken to court and punished. This, however, is impossible, because the responsibility far exceeds the military sphere and implicates a vast spectrum of Argentinian society, including a fair number of those who today cry out, condemning retrospectively the violence to which they too, in one way or another, contributed."[4]

"It would certainly be wonderful": this is the rhetorical trope of false regret, denoting a change from shared indignation at the "atrocious and nauseating" facts, to the more sober realization of what they "really" mean—the impossibility of attaining the "wonderful" goal of impartial justice. Vargas Llosa's is an ancient argument, harking back to notions of original sin: no one soul can truly be held responsible, because every soul is responsible "in one way or another" for the crimes of a nation, whether committed by the people themselves or by their leaders. More than a hundred years ago, Nicolai Gogol expressed the same absurdity in more elegant terms: "Seek out the judge, seek out the criminal, and then condemn both."

Using the case of his own country as a history lesson, Vargas Llosa concluded his *cri de coeur*: "The example of what has happened in Peru, with a democracy which the Peruvian people have distorted—because of the violence of extremist groups and also because of the blindness and demagogy of certain political forces—and which they let fall like a ripe fruit in the arms of military and personal power, should open the eyes of those imprudent justice-seekers who, in Argentina, take advantage of a debate on the repression in the seventies to seek revenge, to avenge old grievances or continue by other means the insane war they started and then lost."

Burson-Marsteller could not have come up with a more efficient publicist for their cause. What would a common reader, confident in Vargas Llosa's intellectual authority, make of this impassioned conclusion? After hesitating, perhaps, at the comparison between Argentina and Peru (where the novelist-turned-politician thunderingly lost the presidential election) which seems to protest too much, too obviously, the reader is led into a far subtler argument: these "justice-seekers"—the seekers of that justice which, according to Vargas Llosa, is desirable but utopian—are they not in fact hypocrites who must not only share the guilt for the atrocities, but are also to blame for starting a war which they then lost? Suddenly the scales of responsibility are tipped ominously to the victims' side. Not a need for justice, not an urge to acknowledge wrongs officially, but an itch for revenge or, even worse, sheer spite, apparently drives these so-called justice-seekers. The thirty thousand disappeared are not to be lamented; they were troublemakers who started it all. And those who survived—the Mothers of Plaza de Mayo, the thousands forced into exile, the hundreds of tortured men and women who crowd the pages of the 1984 *Report on the Disappeared* with their sober accounts of utterly indescribable sufferings—should not seek redress lest they themselves be called to judgement. And furthermore, the seventies are now so long ago ... Would it not be better to forget?

Fortunately, there were readers who were not so confident. Mario Vargas Llosa's article was reprinted in *Le Monde* on 18 May 1995. A week later, the Argentinian writer Juan José Saer published an answer in the same newspaper.[5] After correcting a number of important factual errors in Vargas Llosa's piece—calling Isabel Perón's presidency a "democratic government," ignoring the fact that between 1955 and 1983 Argentina enjoyed barely six years of freely elected leaders—Saer notes that Vargas Llosa's arguments coincide, point by point, with those of the military leaders themselves, who argued that the official tactics of murder and torture had not been their choice but the choice of those who provoked them and forced them to make use of "extreme measures." Saer also points out that Vargas Llosa's notion of "collective responsibility" might place Vargas Llosa himself in a delicate position since, at a time when Argentinian intellectuals were being tortured or forced into exile, the Peruvian novelist continued to publish willingly in Argentina's official press.

Saer responded to Vargas Llosa's role, accusing him of being a spokesman for the military; he dismissed or ignored his arguments, which are based on a number of false assumptions. And yet, since these arguments must stand, thanks to Vargas Llosa's craft, as the most eloquent of those penned by the defenders of a military amnesty, they deserve, perhaps, a closer examination.

- The notion of guilt shared between the military government, which came to power by force and used torture and murder to fight its opposers, and the victims, including guerrilla fighters, political objectors, and ordinary civilians with no political associations, is fallacious. While it could be argued that in a sense the army of insurrectionists and the official Argentinian army were equal forces (though, even here, the numbers appear to be in the order of 1 to 1,000), no argument can find a balance of power between the organized military forces and the intellectuals, artists, union leaders, students, and members of the clergy who expressed disagreement with them. The civilian who voices an objection to the actions of the government is not guilty of any crime; on the contrary, vigilance is an essential civic duty in any democratic society. But the repression overflowed even the realm of civilian opposition. The National Commission on Disappeared People, led by the novelist Ernesto Sábato, concluded its report in September 1984. "We can state categorically—contrary to what the executors of this sinister plan maintain—that they did not pursue only the members of political organizations who carried out acts of terrorism. Among the victims are thousands who never had any links with such activity but were nevertheless subjected to horrific torture because they opposed the military dictatorship, took part in union or student activities, were well-known intellectuals who questioned state terrorism, or simply because they were relatives, friends, or names included in the address book of someone considered subversive."[6]
- Any government that uses torture and murder to enforce the law invalidates both its right to govern and the law it enforces, since one of the few basic tenets of any society in

which citizens are granted equal rights is the sacredness of human life. "Clearly," wrote Chesterton, "there could be no safety for a society in which the remark by the Chief Justice that murder was wrong was regarded as an original and dazzling epigram."[7] Any government that does not recognize this truth, and does not hold accountable those who torture and murder, can make no claims for its own justice. No government can rightly mirror the methods of its criminals, responding in kind to what it might deem an act against the nation's laws. It cannot be guided by an individual sense of justice, or revenge, or greed, or even morality. It must encompass them all, these individual deeds of its citizens, within the parameters established by the country's constitution. It must enforce the law with the law, and within the letter of the law. Beyond the law, a government is no longer a government but a usurped power, and as such it must be judged.

- Trust in the ultimate power of the law sustained many of the military dictatorship's victims during those terrible years. In spite of the pain and the bewilderment caused by the officialized abuses, the belief remained that in a not-too-distant future these acts would be brought to light and judged according to the law. The wish to torture the torturer and to kill the murderer must have been overwhelming, but even stronger was the sense that such acts of revenge would become indistinguishable from the acts that caused them, and would be transformed, in some abominable way, into a victory for the abusers. Instead, the victims and their families continued to believe in some form of ultimate earthly judgement, in which the society that had been wronged would bring the guilty ones to trial according to the laws of that society. Only on the basis of such justice being done did they believe that their country might have another chance. Menem's amnesty denied them that long-awaited possibility.

- This "absence of justice" was reflected with ghoulish symmetry in the "disappearing" tactics employed by the military, by which their victims—kidnapped, tortured, thrown from airplanes, dropped into unmarked graves—became not officially dead but merely "absent," leaving the anguished families with no bodies to mourn. Julio Cortázar, speaking in 1981, described in these words the dictatorship's method: "On the one hand, a virtual or real antagonist is suppressed; on the other, conditions are created so that the family and friends of the victims are often forced to remain silent as the only possibility of preserving the life of those whom their hearts won't allow them to presume dead."[8] And he added, "If every human death entails an irrevocable absence, what can we say of this other absence that continues as a sort of abstract presence, like the obstinate denial of the absence we know to be final?" In that sense, Menem's amnesty doesn't heal the sickness of the past—it merely prolongs that sickness into the present.
- Menem's revisionist attempt is not original. One of the earliest instances of perfecting the present by erasing the tensions of the past took place in the year 213 B.C., when the Chinese emperor Shih Huang-ti ordered that every book in his realm should be thrown to the fire so as to destroy all traces (legend has it) of his mother's adultery. But no deed, however monstrous or trivial, can ever be abolished once committed—not even by a Chinese emperor, even less by an Argentinian president. This is the adamantine law of our life. The immutability of the past does not depend on the volubilities of government, nor on cravings for revenge

or for diplomacy. No deed can be undone. It can be pardoned, but the pardon must come from the offended person and from no one else, if it is to have any emotional validity. Nothing changes in the deed itself after a pardon: not the circumstances, not the gravity, not the guilt, not the wound. Nothing except the relationship between the torturer and the victims, when the victims reaffirm their sovereignty, "not weighing our merits," as the Book of Common Prayer has it, "but by pardoning our offences." Pardon is the victim's prerogative, not the torturer's right—and this Menem's government and his supporters, such as Vargas Llosa, have apparently forgotten.

- The pardon granted by a victim—the dripping quality of mercy—has no bearing on the mechanics of justice. Pardon doesn't change or even qualify the act, which will cast its shadow forward, throughout eternity, into every new present. Pardon doesn't grant oblivion. But a trial, according to the laws of society, can at least lend the criminal act a context; the law can contain it, so to speak, in the past so that it no longer contaminates the future, standing at a distance as a reminder and a warning. In a mysterious way, the application of a society's laws is akin to a literary act: it fixes the criminal deed on a page, defines it in words, gives it a context which is not that of the sheer horror of the moment but of its recollection. The power of memory is no longer in the hands of the criminal; now it is society itself that holds that power, writing the chronicle of its own wicked past, able at last to rebuild itself not over the emptiness of oblivion but over the solid, recorded facts of the atrocities committed. This is a long, dreary, fearful, agonizing process, and the only possible one. This sort of healing always leaves scars.

- Menem's amnesty, bowing to the demands of acknowledged murderers and torturers, has postponed the healing for what appears to be a very long time. As it stands today, Argentina is a country bereft of rights: its right to social justice ignored, its right to moral education invalidated, its right to moral authority forfeit. The need to "carry on," the need to "reconcile differences," the need to "allow the economy to flourish once again" have all been invoked by Menem as good reasons for forgiving and forgetting. Supported by literate voices such as that of Vargas Llosa, Menem apparently believes that history can be paid off; that the memory of thousands of individuals like my friend from school can be left to yellow on forgotten shelves in dim bureaucratic offices; that the past can be recovered without expenditure of effort, without making official amends, without redemption.

While waiting for the act of justice now denied, the victims of Argentina's military dictatorship can still hope for another, older form of justice—less evident, but in the end longer-lasting. The maze of a politician's mind has seldom held the promise of redemption, but that of a gifted writer is almost exclusively built on such a promise, and in spite of Auden's dictum, it allows no forgetting.

Thanks to certain books (a catalogue too long and personal to be of use here) both the torturers and their victims may know that they were not alone, unseen, unassailable. Justice, beyond the requirements of literary conventions that demand a happy end, is in some essential way our common human bond, something against which we can all measure ourselves. As the old English law has it, justice must not only be done but be seen to be done.

Auden's lack of confidence in the writer's ability to change the world is apparently a modern perception. Robert Graves noted that the Irish and Welsh distinguished carefully between poets and satirists: the poet's task was creative or curative, that of the satirist was destructive or noxious, and both changed the course of worldly events.[9] Even nature was supposed to bow to Orpheus's words, and Shakespeare recalled the power of the Irish bards, "rhyming rats to death"; in the seventh century, the great Seanchan Torpest, having discovered that rats had eaten his dinner, slaughtered ten on the spot by uttering a verse that began:

Rats have sharp snouts
Yet are poor fighters.

Whether against rats or dictators, writers can bring about a wild form of justice in their role as God's spies. "Many brave men lived before Agamemnon's time," wrote Horace in the first century B.C., "but they are all, unmourned and unknown, covered by the long night, because they lacked a poet." As Horace implied, we are luckier. Poems and stories that will redeem us (or in which we will find redemption of a kind) are being written, or will be written, or have been written and are awaiting their readers and, throughout time, again and again, assume this: that the human mind is always wiser than its most atrocious deeds, since it can give them a name; that in the very description of our most loathsome acts something in good writing shows them as loathsome and therefore not unconquerable; that in spite of the feebleness and randomness of language, an inspired writer can tell the unspeakable and lend a shape to the unthinkable, so that evil loses some of its numinous quality and stands reduced to a few memorable words.

[1] Reprinted in *Harper's*, New York, July 1995 (trans. by Alex Frankel).

[2] This figure is the estimate of the National Commission on Disappeared People, quoted in *Nunca Más (Never Again): A Report by Argentina's National Commission on Disappeared People*, ed. and trans. by Nick Caistor, Faber & Faber; and in *Index on Censorship*, London, 1986.

[3] R. Scott Greathead, "Truth in Argentina," *The New York Times*, 11 May 1995.

[4] Mario Vargas Llosa, "Jouer avec le feu," *Le Monde*, Paris, 18 May 1995.

[5] Juan José Saer, "Mario Vargas Llosa au-delà de l'erreur," *Le Monde*, Paris, 26 mai 1995.

[6] *Nunca Más (Never Again): A Report by Argentina's National Commission on Disappeared People*, ed. and trans. by Nick Caistor, Faber & Faber and *Index on Censorship*, London, 1986.

[7] G. K. Chesterton, "A Defence of Penny Dreadfuls" in *The Defendant*, London, 1901.

[8] Julio Cortázar, "Negación del olvido" in *Obra Crítica*, vol. 3, ed. Saúl Sasnowski, Alfaguara, Madrid, 1983.

[9] Robert Graves, *The White Goddess: Amended and Enlarged Edition*, New York, 1996.

The Age of Revenge

Life being what it is, one dreams of revenge.

PAUL GAUGUIN

1. On the third Arabian Night, Scheherazade tells this story:

A FISHERMAN, OLD AND VERY POOR, was in the habit of casting his nets no more than four times a day. One evening, after casting his nets three times and pulling out nothing except mud and stones, he begged God to forgive his impatience and to remember that the next casting would be the last of the day. Then the fisherman threw his nets out for the fourth and last time. The nets felt heavy, and when he pulled them in he saw that he had netted a small copper bottle. Curious to see what it contained, the fisherman picked the lid off with his knife and shook out the bottle's contents. To his amazement, a thick smoke poured forth, collected into a cloud and formed the figure of a colossal efreet or genie who towered over the fisherman and said: "I am one of the heretical djinns whom King Suleiman imprisoned in a bottle as a punishment for not submitting to his will. Cast in my prison to the bottom of the sea, I remained there for one thousand years, and promised to whoever would free me all the riches in the world—but no one came. For the next one thousand years, I promised him who would save me all the wisdom in the world—but still no one came. For the third one thousand years I promised him who would deliver me to perform any three wishes—and still no one came. I then fell into a violent rage, and said to myself, Whoever frees me now, I shall kill. Prepare then to die, Oh my saviour!"

Maybe we too have reached that fourth millennium, the point when patience comes to an end. Now, with the advantage of hindsight, it's obvious that we had every indication that this would happen. Our history, everywhere and at all times, has been one of such abuse, such injustice, such cruelty, that reading through it I wonder why the cesspool of hatred we have produced as a result hasn't yet welled up and drowned us. For centuries and centuries, just like the genie, the victims have told their victimizers: let us be free and we'll all prosper, let us be vocal and we'll all become wise, let us be equal and we'll all try to live together in some sort of rational harmony. But not any longer. Now, finally, the victims have decided that the time for patience is over. Remember the title of James Baldwin's book, *The Fire Next Time*? This is the next time.

One of the many ways in which the fiction we call history can be visualized—as Ariel and Willy Durant naively imagined—is through the typical moods of each so-called period, through the sense that apparently permeates a decade, a century, an age—the Age of Reason, the Age of Uncertainty, and so on. For our time, for this "end of the millennium," I believe that the prevailing sentiment would force us to call this the Age of Revenge. Now, louder and louder, millions of voices seem to be saying, "It's our turn." They are not pleading, they are not trying to convince, they are not even demanding justice. They are simply torching their way to the front. They are certainly not using the fire to enlighten anyone. They fight intolerance with intolerance. And they want no camaraderie.

I am not an advocate of tolerance in the sense in which we've often used the word. ("We must be tolerant of homosexuals, because their sexuality is in an arrested state," pleaded a leading Argentinian psychiatrist in 1992; "We must tolerate the Jews or they will declare themselves the world's martyrs," argued Martin Heidegger in 1933.) Tolerance, which in the past usually implied an anti-hierarchical stance, now often implies a hierarchy, someone condescending "to be tolerant" of someone else and demanding gratitude for it. Tolerance is a kind of philanthropy that ends up by consuming itself. "Tolerance," wrote E. M. Forster in *Two Cheers for Democracy*, "merely means putting up with people, being able to stand things." But intolerance too is self-destructive. Intolerance (as the genie found out) is a form of suicide.

In this sense, both tolerance and intolerance reject the notion of equality. You cannot be tolerant—or even intolerant—towards someone you perceive as possessing identical rights and responsibilities as yourself. Our history, in spite of the brave motto of the French Revolution, seems to confirm this. We appear to be condemned by arrangements, or disarrangements, made before we were born, and of which we are the heirs, whether we want it or not. History would have us believe that the fisherman is condemned to the traditional tricks of his abused class, as Solomon and the genie were to theirs, inheritors of their roles as king and slave. In *The Muse of History*, the poet Derek Walcott says, "But who in the New World does not have a horror of the past, whether his ancestor was torturer or victim? Who, in the depth of conscience, is not silently screaming for pardon or revenge?"

Intolerance breeds intolerance. After General Perón demoted Borges from librarian to poultry inspector at a municipal market, Borges said the following: "Dictatorships breed oppression, dictatorships breed servility, dictatorships breed cruelty; more abominable is the fact that they breed stupidity." Intolerance is a form of stupidity, in the sense that it is unable to see individual richness and is only able to deal in stereotypes. It belongs in the same category as prejudice, whereby rational process is supplanted by a cliché, an *idée reçue*.

And yet intolerance, like the genie's response, comes from people at their wit's end. We may not feel guilty for the sins of our fathers, or even for those of our contemporaries, but because the established rule is to identify individuals by the characteristics of a predetermined group—the method of racism—those individuals in turn identify us in exactly the same way. Such stereotypes are always bred from ignorance. And ignorance, as Montesquieu put it, is the mother of tradition. For Solomon, the genie is traditionally just one of the slaves; for the genie, Solomon is just one of the oppressors. Because for centuries blacks were seen as herds of cattle by the members of white society, the members of white society are seen (Louis Farrakhan's description) as "a pack of wolves" by blacks, and every act that affects the blacks is seen as part of an overarching racist attitude. Our society has established generalities as the norm, and now generalities *are* the norm. "The norm is never normal," wrote the Aboriginal novelist Mudrooroo.

Up to a certain degree, prejudice is a question of pronouns. The stress of "We" is exclusive; that is to say, "We" means "Not you."

All good people agree,
    And all good people say,
All nice people, like Us, are We
    And every one else is They:

But if you cross over the sea,
Instead of over the way,
You may end by (think of it!) looking on We
As only a sort of They!

This was written by Rudyard Kipling in 1919.

What those in power seem to forget is that the formation of any group for the purpose of exclusion—blacks, women, Jews, gays, any segregated ethnic or national group you may care to think of—instantly grants that group the selfsame methods. By excluding someone from us, we exclude ourselves from that someone. When we say "you are not us" we are also saying "we are not you."

The same can be said of the books we read. The act of reading lends us a peculiar kind of knowledge, which can result in a transformation of the surrounding world and of ourselves, can mysteriously effect a profound epistemological change; or else it is an action in itself, a sort of Moebius strip of experience, endlessly stroking its single side. For Shelley, poetry laid out the laws by which we understand the world; for Tristan Tzara, poetry had no role to play except to distract us from the world. Shelley was right in that we, the readers, can make sense of the chaos of the world through those scribbles; Tzara was right in that a poem is nothing but the scribbles on a page.

I myself have always seen literature, its conversion through the act of reading, as a process of expansion in which the text becomes a palimpsest as I read through its words the many layers of my other readings. Even if this has had no immediate, visible effect on our society, I still believe in the effectiveness of the "scribbles," because they empower the reader to act differently—to read "revenge," for instance, where another has written "forceful pursuit of justice." Literature redefines itself out of its own materials, not by rejecting but by rereading, and I suggest that our task is to keep proposing new points of view, so that the presences and absences from which we now suffer can be more clearly seen—and to afford them ultimately their proper and common place.

But are there limits to this process of redefinition, to the renewed use we can make of these scribbles? A classic example may be useful here. Joseph Conrad's *Heart of Darkness* has been read by Chinua Achebe as a racist text, in spite of its literary merit, so much so that Achebe says he is appalled that such a text can be considered an "English classic." All the elements Achebe recognizes as racist are, certainly, in Conrad's novel. For instance:

Marlow, the narrator, is describing a crowd of African people: "a mass of naked, breathing, quivering, bronze bodies." In the front are three men, "plastered with bright red earth from head to foot."

> They faced the river, stamped their feet, nodded their horned heads, swayed their scarlet bodies; they shook towards the fierce river-demon a bunch of black feathers, a mangy skin with a pendant tail—something that looked like a dried gourd; they shouted periodically together strings of amazing words that resembled no sounds of human language; and the deep murmurs of the crowd, interrupted suddenly, were like the responses of some satanic litany.

Compare this to another example, taken from a less classic text:

> Mark Brendon was old-fashioned and the women born of the war attracted him not at all. He recognized their fine

> qualities and often their distinction of mind; yet his ideal struck backward to another and earlier type—the type of his own mother who, as a widow, had kept house for him until her death. She was his feminine ideal—restful, sympathetic, trustworthy—one who always made his interests hers, one who concentrated upon his life rather than her own and found in his progress and triumphs the core of her own existence.
>
> Mark wanted, in truth, somebody who would be content to merge herself in him and seek neither to impress her own personality upon his, nor develop an independent environment. He had wit to know that a mother's standpoint must be vastly different from that of any wife, no matter how perfect her devotion; he had experience enough of married men to doubt whether the woman he sought was to be found in a post-war world; yet he preserved and permitted himself a hope that the old-fashioned women still existed, and he began to consider where he might find such a helpmate.

The source is one of the most famous of the British detective novels of the Golden Age, Eden Phillpotts' *The Red Redmaynes*, published in 1920.

As a reader, I can make any number of choices. The elements of the text—according to my reading tone, sense of humour, experience, knowledge of context, and more—can be transformed in a number of different ways by what Giovanna Franci calls *L'ansia dell'interpretazione*, the anxious desire to interpret. Umberto Eco, in *The Limits of Interpretation*, suggests that the "open" interpretation, what he once called "the cancer of uncontrolled interpretation," is limited by the reader's common sense; that there is a basic common response to a text, a response that allows for a modicum of communication.

In the case of Conrad, for instance, the "racist" reading of *Heart of Darkness* is of course possible. And yet I don't believe it is a useful one. Essentially, at the heart of darkness is not Africa, or the white man's vision of Africa, or the black savages described in the offensive passage. At the heart of darkness is Kurtz. "His soul was mad," says Marlow. "Being alone in the wilderness, it had looked within itself and, by heavens! I tell you, it had gone mad. I had—for my sins, I suppose—to go through the ordeal of looking into it myself. No eloquence could have been so withering to one's belief in mankind as his final burst of sincerity." The whole point is that Kurtz, and Marlow eventually, and we all, must go through the ordeal of looking into ourselves. And because we live in the world we live in, we won't do it amidst noble thoughts of human equality, mutual respect, or even love for one another. We have to do it in this cesspool we have created, among cries of murder and revenge. It would be arrogant of me to deny Achebe's experience as a reader—and the racist passages are there, and belong to and define Kurtz's world, and the world of Marlow, and of many of Conrad's admirers—you and I. But whether this does or does not reflect Conrad's own point of view is something that now only bears discussion in a fine and private place. In the text, the question is not relevant, because Conrad (whoever he was) is not part of the discourse of *Heart of Darkness*. Those black savages are still the image perceived by the vast majority of our neighbours, by white juries in Los Angeles, by policemen in Toronto, by anti-immigration lobbyists in Australia, by honest citizens in the French countryside. "Do you understand this?" cries Marlow to Kurtz at the end. "Do I not?" is Kurtz's answer. He later dies, probably believing that he does understand. And Marlow, who remains faithful to Kurtz to the last, "and even beyond," probably believes it too. He will also die, somewhere outside the novel, believing that great lie of imperialism, that the victimizer is ultimately the victim. What makes *Heart of Darkness* a great novel—despite what Achebe sees—is that it doesn't gloss over this horror: not the horror seen by Kurtz but the horror of the entire world, made by the whole of humankind, Europe and Africa both. In that sense, *Heart of Darkness* seems to me a remarkable denunciation of racism, in which there is no hope within the system as it stands. And whether Conrad believed it or not is irrelevant. A great work of art is always superior to its creator. "There is hope, but not for us," said Kafka. That could be the epigraph of *Heart of Darkness.*

The quotation from *The Red Redmaynes* asks other questions. First, how did the book's earliest readers react to this passage? Presumably without surprise or humour. Though a few readers would, perhaps, have felt otherwise, it is extraordinary to think how unremarkable this passage must have seemed to the common reader in the 1920s. But second, for a reader today, what significance does the passage have? Other than to justify the anger of being reduced to what Phillpotts calls a "helpmate," would it not allow us a starting-point to explore the broader literary assumptions of the period? Nineteen twenty-two was the year Joyce published *Ulysses.* Who is Molly Bloom in relation to our Phillpotts' *Ewig-Weibliche*? I leave the question unanswered.... And as far as my readings of both Conrad and Phillpotts are concerned, I must agree with Tzara. I read these scribbles and outside, in the world of dust and bricks, nothing has changed. Injustice is still injustice, as the daily papers tell us.

And yet....

Even though a text itself allows for any number of readings, it is apparent that the groups in power, defined in contrast to the groups they exploit, largely determine the accepted reading. Male over female, white over black, straight over gay, have been the norms for at least the genie's last three millennia. In recent times, it has been suggested that the texts themselves are to blame. That the creation of texts by other hands, in other voices, will shift the emphasis, and that certain voices, which have been speaking about matters that directly concern the oppressed groups, should voluntarily keep quiet for a while and provide room to those who, among the oppressed, have been denied access.

This is the American writer Alice Walker:

What can the white man say to the black woman?
Only one thing that the black woman might hear.

. . . .

I will remove myself as an obstacle in the path that your
    children,
against all odds,
are making towards the light. I will not assassinate them
for dreaming dreams and
offering new visions of how to live. I will cease trying to
    lead your children,
for I
can see I have never understood where I was going.
I will agree to sit quietly for a
century or so, and meditate on this.

This is what the white man can say to the black woman.
We are listening.

How can I argue with the poetic logic of Walker's text? But I would like to make a suggestion. There is no doubt that more oppressed voices should and must be heard. There is no doubt that more Alice Walkers, James Baldwins, Mudrooroos need to come to the surface. But unless there is a whole new breed of readers to take those texts upon themselves, to read in them "new visions of how to live," not much will change. It is on the readers that we must concentrate, not on the writers, on the readers who will make use of the text and "make something happen." Unless this education of the reader occurs, no number of new voices will change anything, because they will echo among a deaf crowd. And if these readers learn to seek out, to interpret, to translate, to put texts into a variety of contexts, to transform the texts through multiple layers of reading—if we, readers, train ourselves to do this—then we won't need any voices to be silenced, because we will be able to make choices. A silenced voice, whether silenced voluntarily or not, never disappears. Its absence becomes enormous, too enormous to ignore. Surely it's not another absence we want, another vacuum for a hundred or a thousand years, but a period of redress, in which those voices come up and share the audibility that for so long those in power have usurped.

I am also convinced that hope lies with individuals, and that solutions don't lie in crowds. One of the greatest triumphs of any oppressor is to convert the oppressed to his methods. A reader need not embrace a writer's methods, or even those of another reader. A text allows in itself more freedom than we usually think possible, which is why governments are never really keen on literacy, and why it is usually writers and seldom deep-sea divers or stockbrokers who are imprisoned, tortured and killed for political reasons.

But the story of the genie in the bottle has a counterpart.

During the military dictatorship in Argentina in the seventies, the poet Juan Gelman, who was then in his mid-forties, was forced to escape to Spain. His son and daughter-in-law, however, were captured by the military, tortured and killed. The daughter-in-law was pregnant. Gelman was informed of all this while in exile in Spain. A year or so later, one of Gelman's friends met him in Spain, and told him the name of the one man directly responsible for the death of Gelman's son and daughter-in-law. Gelman decided to return to Argentina and kill him. Friends tried to convince him not to go, but he felt that his life had no more meaning, and that revenge would somehow mitigate the absence or appease the memory of his dead. Gelman returned to Argentina with a false passport, but before he could look for the murderer he was visited by two women. These women, who had been informed of his coming by Gelman's friends, told him that they belonged to the Mothers of Plaza de Mayo, mothers whose children had been "disappeared" by the military and who assembled, week after week, in front of the presidential palace, to show that their sons and daughters had not been forgotten. The women wanted to talk to Gelman. I don't know what they said to him, but the gist of it was that if Gelman killed the murderer of his son and daughter-in-law, he would in effect become one of "them," he would in effect betray the memory of both his son and his daughter-in-law. I don't know what words they used or how their argument was reasoned, but in the end Gelman agreed, and returned to Spain.

I don't think I would be capable. If someone did anything to one of my children, I can very easily see myself turning into a murderer, literature or no literature, and I can't imagine an argument that would dissuade me. But there *was* an argument.

And these women put it forward. And in the case of Gelman, it achieved something better than mere revenge. And that, I believe, is another possible reading.

VIII

CERTAIN BOOKS

"Now I declare that's too bad!" Humpty Dumpty cried, breaking into a sudden passion. "You've been listening at doors—and behind trees—and down chimneys—or you couldn't have known it!"

"I haven't indeed!" Alice said very gently. "It's in a book."

Through the Looking-Glass, Chapter VI

Taking Chesterton at His Word

Names are everything. I never quarrel with actions.
My one quarrel is with words.
That is the reason I hate vulgar realism in literature.

OSCAR WILDE,
The Picture of Dorian Gray

READING CHESTERTON, we are overwhelmed by a remarkable sense of happiness. His prose is the opposite of academic: it is joyful. Words bounce and spark lights off one another as if a clockwork toy had suddenly come to life, clicking and whirring with common sense, that most surprising of marvels. Language was to him a construction box with which to build toy theatres and toy weapons and, as Christopher Morley has noted, "his play upon words often led to a genuine play upon thoughts." There is something rich and detailed, colourful and noisy in his writing. So-called English sobriety didn't suit him, neither in dress (his vast floating cloak, his battered pudding-pot hat and gnomic pince-nez made him look like a pantomime figure) nor in words (he kept worrying and teasing a sentence until it unfolded like a flowering vine, branching off in several directions with tropical gusto, blooming into several ideas at once). He wrote and read with the passion a glutton brings to eating and drinking, but probably with more enjoyment, and the sufferings of the scribbler bent over Mallarmé's blank page never seem to have been his, nor the anguish of the scholar surrounded by ancient tomes. Reading a book was for Chesterton rather a physical than an intellectual act. Father John O'Connor, the model for his Father Brown, said that when Chesterton read a book "he turned it inside out, dog-eared it, pencilled it, sat on it, took it to bed and rolled on it, and got up again and spilled tea on it—if he were sufficiently interested." And he wrote with equal brio, overflowing his seat at a beer-stained table in a smoky café on Fleet Street. One of the Italian waiters there described him like this: "He very clever man. He sit and laugh. And then he write. And then he laugh at what he write."

From his first collection of essays, *The Defendant*, published in 1901 when Chesterton was 27, he appeared to be a man in a constant state of wonder: not a solemn, meditative state in which the mind sluggishly unravelled an idea across ruled pages and through numbered ledgers, but a state in which the mind flitted about, attracted here and distracted there, joyful and constantly surprised. "What was wonderful about childhood," Chesterton wrote in his *Autobiography*, "is that anything in it was a wonder. It was not merely a world full of miracles; it was a miraculous world. What gives me this shock is almost anything I really recall; not the things I should think most worth recalling." This was a gift he seems to have possessed throughout his life. Everything he "really" recalled became worthy of meditation. No subject seemed beyond his reach, if not his interest. Whatever the question, and however serious, Chesterton refused to be solemn, especially when being serious. In a letter to his wife-to-be, Frances Blogg, earnestly discussing the nature of domesticity, he wrote:

> My idea ... is to make a house really allegoric: really explain its own essential meaning. Mystical or ancient sayings should be inscribed on every object, the more prosaic the object the better. "Hast thou sent Rain upon the Earth?" should be inscribed on the Umbrella-Stand: perhaps on the Umbrella. "Even the Hairs of your Head are all numbered" would give tremendous significance to one's hairbrushes: the words about "living water" would reveal the music and sanctity of the sink: while "Our God is a consuming Fire" might be written over the kitchen-grate, to assist the mystical musings of the cook.

Because what mattered to him were the connections and reactions between facts, not the facts themselves, accuracy—in the documentary sense of the word—was of no importance to him. He had no patience with what he called the "fairness of intellect" that made him despair of an earnest man's soul. He understood that nothing much changed in his reflections on French history if he discovered that Napoleon had been born in 1768 instead of 1769—or at least that the exact year was not as important to Chesterton as the general's shortness of height and of temper, upon either of which he could reflect with enjoyment and profit. In his amusing biography of Robert Browning, written for the very serious series "English Men of Letters," not only did he misquote the poet himself, but he even invented a line for one of Browning's most famous poems, "Mr. Sludge the Medium." When Chesterton's *Dickens* appeared, George Bernard Shaw wrote him a long letter listing a whole pack of howlers. Chesterton was unmoved, and in recent years, one of Dickens's latest biographers, Peter Ackroyd, hailed Chesterton, in spite of such errors, as the finest of Dickensian critics.

He had begun writing at school; by the time he was twenty, without a break and hardly a change of style, he was contributing articles about almost anything to a number of London magazines such as *The Bookman* and *The Speaker*. (Though in his *Autobiography* he mentions beginning at the *Academy* in 1895, there are no traces of his reviews in that magazine that year; later the *Academy* peevishly wrote that Chesterton's books were "always and inevitably a bore.") About these early talents he was characteristically dismissive: "Having entirely failed to learn how to draw or paint, I tossed off easily enough some criticisms of the weaker points of Rubens or the misdirected talents of Tintoretto. I had discovered the easiest of all professions, which I have pursued ever since."

His views of society were anti-aristocratic and vaguely akin to those of the former British Liberal Party: he believed in honest shopkeepers, decent poor and corrupt rich whom he saw as greedy camels lumbering towards the twinkling eye of a needle. He vigorously attacked the arrogance of those who in the name of superior funds, blood or education dictated to the "lower classes" (meaning "humanity minus ourselves") in an effort to reform their lives. He made fun of the censoring judges who wanted to brand cheap adventure novels as "criminal and degrading": "This is magisterial theory," he noted, "and this is rubbish." He thumbed his nose at the egotism and aloofness of the rich: "Among the Very Rich you will never find a really generous man, even by accident. They may give their money away, but they will never give themselves away." He pointed fingers at the philanthropic politicians who believed they knew better than the people what was good for the people: This belief, he wrote, is "the most poisonous of all the political wrongs that rot out the entrails of the world." And he summed up all these high and mighty characters as citizens of nations going mad. "They have grown used to their own unreason; chaos is their cosmos; and the whirlwind is the breath of their nostrils. These nations are really in danger of going off their heads *en masse*; of becoming one vast vision of imbecility, with toppling cities and crazy country-sides, all dotted with industrious lunatics." Then, with a Chestertonian flourish, he threw down his *j'accuse*: "One of these countries is modern England."

In his essays, as in his fictions, this vigorous sense of social justice propels the story. His fictions, extensions of his essays, consist of neatly constructed plots that begin with a mysterious horror and an unnatural ticking, and end (all but the masterful *Man Who Was Thursday*) with a reasonable resolution that somehow, in its very simplicity, heightens the suspected horror. His essays themselves tell stories in which most of the characters, except perhaps the author himself, are mere sketches, cogs in the memorable plot. With Borges, Chesterton could say of his writings: "They are not, they don't attempt to be, psychological." What matters are the arguments and words bringing the story into being through the devices of a personal rhetoric, and the clicking together of episodes into an exquisite and logical arch, held aloft merely through the perfect joining of its parts. In Chesterton's writings, emotion and reason—those artificially separated Siamese twins—are again one. For instance: the emotion provoked by the sight, in a London court of justice, of a woman who has "neglected her children" is perfectly expressed in its riposte, "and who looked as if someone or something had neglected her." Or the anger provoked by two policeman questioning him for playing with a knife in the woods, and then letting him go because he was a guest at a rich man's house, leads him to conclude: "The inference seems painfully clear: either it is not a proof of infamy to throw a knife about in a lonely wood, or else it is a proof of innocence to know a rich man." This is not merely clever: this feels true, to sense and to sound.

In the ancient dispute between content and form, or sense and sound, Chesterton stood halfway. He only partly followed the Duchess, who had admonished Alice: "Take care of the sense and the sounds will take care of themselves." Sense, Chesterton believed, could, if properly sought, exploit the *effects* of sound and rise unbidden from the clashing of rhetorical cymbals—from oxymoron and paradox, from hyperbole and metonymy. Chesterton was more inclined to agree with Pope, who once compared the followers of mere sound to those who attend church "not for the doctrine, but the music there" (*An Essay on Criticism*, 1771). Chesterton loved the music of words, but realized their limited ability to signify: whatever doctrine they might announce must needs be incomplete, haphazard glimmers rather than flashes of truth. In his study of the painter Watts he wrote:

> Every religion and every philosophy must, of course, be based on the assumption of the authority or the accuracy of something. But it may well be questioned whether it is not saner and more satisfactory to ground our faith on the infallibility of the Pope, or the infallibility of the Book of Mormon, than on this astounding modern dogma of the infallibility of human speech. Every time one man says to another, "Tell us plainly what you mean?" he is assuming the infallibility of language: this is to say, he is assuming that there is a perfect scheme of verbal expression for all the internal moods and meanings of men. Whenever a man says to another, "Prove your case; defend your faith," he is assuming the infallibility of language: that is to say,

> he is assuming that a man has a word for every reality in earth, or heaven, or hell. He knows that there are in the soul tints more bewildering, more numberless, and more nameless than the colours of an autumn forest; he knows that there are abroad in the world and doing strange and terrible service in it crimes that have never been condemned and virtues that have never been christened. Yet he seriously believes that these things can every one of them, in all their tones and semi-tones, in all their blends and unions, be accurately represented by an arbitrary system of grunts and squeals. He believes that an ordinary civilized stockbroker can really produce out of his own inside noises which denote all the mysteries of memory and all the agonies of desire.

Paradoxically, in words like these, written against the power of words, Chesterton raises the reader's trust in that same questioned power.

What gave coherence to his eclectic curiosity, and provided him with a unified mythology and vocabulary, was the Catholic Church. Its vast intricacies allowed him a verbal caper that stern Protestantism would have frowned on. And confronted with the *dépouillement* of Cromwell's temples, his rumbustious soul was joyfully drawn to the gold and pink and white of Rome, which he saw as depicting the Church's great optimism. "Jesus Christ was crucified," he remarked, "not because of anything he said about God, but on a charge of saying that a man could in three days pull down and rebuild the Temple." And added: "Every one of the great revolutionists, from Isaiah to Shelley, have been optimists." In his late twenties, the numinous became his grammar, and after his marriage to Frances Blogg (a Roman Catholic and an assiduous church-goer), he found in the strictures of ritual and the mysteries of the Old Religion a context and a purpose to his prose and a sense to the world. "The world is a problem, not a theorem," he wrote, "And the word of the last day will be Q.E.F."—"Which was to be done."

As an adolescent, brought up an Anglican, he had suddenly found himself in a mood of seemingly fathomless morbidity, which he later called a state of "moral anarchy." This bleakness expressed itself in "an overpowering impulse to record or draw horrible ideas and images; plunging deeper and deeper as in a blind spiritual suicide" which lasted intermittently until his conversion. What exactly these ideas and images might have been we don't know, but it isn't impossible that a shadow, an echo, well after he had become a Catholic, found its way into his later work—in the horrors listed, for instance, in *The Man Who Was Thursday*, such as the man "who had dreamed all night of falling over precipices and had woke up in the morning when he was to be hanged" or the face that seemed so big as one approached it that it filled one with the fear that in the end "it might be too big to be possible." These became, like the inaccurate facts in his essays, accurate inklings of what Chesterton called "the dark side of the heart."

But there is a bleaker side in his writings of which he seems not to have had any inkling at all. It is impossible to read Chesterton thoroughly and not come across clumsy anti-Semitic, antifeminist and racist remarks that wear lightly the same rhetorical devices that make his essays intelligent, moving and brilliant. It is as if a deeper, uglier side of society's collective madness suddenly held sway, forcing the writer to pay a debt to his time and to those in power in his time, overpowering the language of recollection, making his words stilted, superficial, obscene. These are the moments when one senses that his fruitful memory, the epiphany of wonder that he said was at the source of his imagination, comes not from Chesterton himself, the individual, but from the man of his age, from the member of the class that spoke derisively of "our friends the Israelites," of "the primitive Negroes" and of "the weaker sex." Then his eclectic politics lose their individuality, paradox becomes contradiction, and his *bons mots* read as mere conservative slogans. He spoke against Hitler but made ugly anti-Jewish pronouncements:

I am fond of Jews
Jews are fond of money
Never mind whose
I am fond of Jews
Oh, but when they lose
Damn it all, it's funny.

He opposed the imperialistic Boer War at a time when even Shaw and H. G. Wells were for it, but his anti-imperialism stemmed from the belief that nothing foreign could be part of England; English minds would not be broadened, he thought, "by the study of Wagga-Wagga and Timbuctoo." He passionately believed in every person's free will but laughed at women's efforts to become free: "Twenty million young women rose to their feet with the cry 'we will not be dictated to' and proceeded to become stenographers." Funny as the phrasing may be, the joke is spoiled by being spoken in an age of brutal suffragette repression, late and voracious imperialism and the rise of the Third Reich. And here language no longer rings true. Chesterton must have known this, since he himself wrote, in admirable contradiction to these utterings, of the implied moral danger: "There is a terrible Circean law in the background that if the soul stoops too ostentatiously to examine anything it never gets up again."

There are writers who, in their most compassionate, sensitive passages of writing, read like *poseurs*; only in their vilest remarks do they seem humane: Lautréamont, for instance, describing the deliberate torture of a child and Jonathan Swift, in his brutal satires. Others, for all their ranting, let their humanity be seen almost unwillingly, as a slip or a mistake, in their very misanthropy: Léon Bloy, Ezra Pound, Philip Larkin. There is something contrived about their tantrums. Chesterton belongs to neither sort: instead, he will refute himself, again and again, with deadly accuracy. Once, when his adversary at a debate failed to make an appearance, Chesterton took both stands and argued brilliantly both for and against the question of the evening. In the same way, his most bigoted remarks are demolished by his own arguments a few pages later. The man who makes fun of a man for being black or of a woman for wanting independence, is the same man who writes: "I can well imagine a man cutting his throat merely because he has stood by and seen a woman stripped and scourged quite late in the history of England and Ireland, or some negro burnt alive as he still is in the United States. But some part of this shocking shame lies in us all."

It is curious that, for such a fruitful and thought-provoking writer, Chesterton should have had almost no followers. The English once read him and then forgot him or shelved him among the ancients; the French admired him (admire him still) but at a distance. One of the few writers who consciously adopted Chesterton's voice was Borges. Borges devoured and digested Chesterton, and paid him the homage of retelling him in Spanish, modelling on the Father Brown stories his own detective fictions and applying to his essays the Chestertonian style of discourse. In 1960, Borges wrote a short fable, "The Plot," in which the fate of Julius Caesar, who dies uttering the words "You too, my son!" directed to his best-beloved Brutus, is compared to the fate of an Argentinian gaucho, cornered and knifed by a handful of other gauchos. As he falls, he recognizes among the assailants his godson and says "with gentle reproach and unhurried surprise" (Borges adds the warning: "These words must be heard, not read"), "*Pero, che!*" The story ends: "He is killed and he doesn't know he must die for a scene to be repeated." "*Pero, che!*" is untranslatable, except that some forty years earlier Chesterton, searching for a comparison, had written: "As if Caesar's '*Et tu, Brute*' might be translated, 'What, *you* here?'" Borges's Argentinian expression exactly reflects that laconic incredulity.

That events and their causes change according to the telling, mirroring common features or dark oceans of difference; that our understanding of the world may depend on the arrangement of words on a page and on the inflection given to those words; that words, in the end, are all we have to defend ourselves with and that the worth of words, like that of our mortal selves, lies in their very fallibility and elegant brittleness—all this Chesterton knew and incessantly recorded. Whether we have to courage to agree with him is, obviously, another matter.

The Irresolutions of Cynthia Ozick

Fiction is all discovery....
Essays know too much.

CYNTHIA OZICK,
Foreword to *Art & Ardor*

CHILDREN KNOW WHAT most adults have forgotten: that reality is whatever seems real to us. That though the external world cannot be denied (as Dr. Johnson demonstrated by kicking a stone) it can be relighted and rearranged to mean anything we choose. The rules for the creation of our individual realities are magic rules: they depend on belief and must be obeyed with utter rigour and seriousness. Writers have in common with children and lunatics these quotidian acts of creation which, at their best, come to stand for our accepted view of the world. Dickens is the author of Victorian London, and Mark Twain created the Mississippi.

In 1985, I was preparing a CBC radio series (never completed) on the pretentious theme of the Writer and God. My list of writers included Bernard Malamud, Borges (who told me that of God's literary tastes we can know nothing), Elie Wiesel, Angela Carter (who roared with laughter into the microphone after my first question, said she had no idea what I was on about, and happily put an end to the interview) and Cynthia Ozick.

Ozick arrived at the studio looking slightly incongruous: short, shy, a Richard III haircut framing a pair of dark-rimmed glasses. "I'm divided in two," she said, and then, as if apologizing, "Most people are." She explained, "Half of me is a citizen who lives in the world, and half of me is a writer. The citizen has one relationship with God, and the writer has an entirely different one. As a citizen I am awed by Deuteronomy 29:29, which says, 'The secret things belong unto the Lord our God; but those things which are revealed belong to us and to our children for ever.' As a citizen, I am not allowed to reflect upon those secret, mystical things. I am a Jew; I must therefore be agnostic. But as a writer, I can't. As a writer I am gnostic, and the unknown is my wonderful meat and drink." Later she extended the definition: "I am a pagan. The writer in me flies from God and goes to the gods."

In Judaism, only God is the Creator. Creation by a hand other than God's would seriously infringe on His essential unity. God is a jealous Author who admits no competition. The Divine Craftsman, the Demiurge of the Platonists, must be One. But among the pagan gods there is always room for one more: the divine craftsmen are many.

The theme of creation (who creates? what is created? how does creation take place?) runs through Ozick's work like a scarlet thread. It makes her wonder, in her superb books of essays, such as *Art & Ardor* and *Metaphor & Memory*, how writers and readers create their fictional worlds. It leads her in exquisite long and short stories (collected, for instance, in *The Pagan Rabbi* and *The Puttermesser Papers*) to the visionary activities of her characters. It takes her, in her novel *The Cannibal Galaxy*, into the budding groves of parenthood and education. It forces her, in *The Messiah of Stockholm*, to build an infinite progression of creations, of literary chickens and eggs.

Ozick's essays often stem from a review, usually for the book pages of the *New York Times* and the *New Republic*. Most reviewers, in my experience, make the reader wonder: what in the world is the use of these self-appointed Virgils who pretend to guide us through this hell of a novel or that purgatory of a memoir? Who needs someone reading over our shoulder, giggling, sobbing or going into raptures of glee or disgust? Nothing can replace our own reading, and yet the preamble or postface to a text that a reviewer provides can, and in some cases does, turn a book on its head in a refreshing and illuminating way. For me, this has always been the case when reading one of Ozick's reviews.

Take, for example, Ozick's review of Primo Levi's *The Drowned and the Saved*, included in *Metaphor & Memory*. First she gives the bare facts: who Primo Levi was ("an Italian Jewish chemist from Turin"), the peculiarities of his life ("he was liberated from Auschwitz by a Soviet military unit in January of 1945, when he was 25"), and what his written work consisted of ("from that moment of reprieve ... until shortly before his death in April of 1987, he went on recalling, examining, reasoning, recording—telling the ghastly tale—in book after book"). So far, so good. But immediately after this Ozick makes her first leap. She quotes the Coleridge epigraph Levi chose for his last book:

> Since then, at an uncertain hour
> That agony returns,
> And till my ghastly tale is told
> This heart within me burns.

And, after commenting that these words "have never before rung out with such an antimetaphorical contemporary demand, or seemed so cruel," Ozick concludes that Levi's death, hurling himself down a spiral staircase four stories deep, must have been suicide. "The composition of that last Lager manuscript was complete, the heart burned out; there was no more to tell."

Now, readers owe no justifications to anyone except themselves, and then only upon demand. But a reviewer is a reader once removed, guiding the reader, not through the book, but through the reviewer's reading of that book. So Ozick needs to explain her explanation.

The way she does this is by counterpointing by shadow-reading. She quotes Levi on the suicide of another Jewish writer, Jean Améry, also a victim of the Nazis. Levi assumed that Améry took his life as a belated consequence of "trading punches" with a Polish criminal in the concentration camp. "Those who 'trade blows' with the entire world," wrote Levi, "achieve dignity but pay a very high price for it because they are sure to be defeated." This, Ozick says pointedly, must be borne in mind when approaching Levi's suicide. Because, as storytellers know, every story has another side which the storyteller does not always see. And, through an association of quotations from and reflections on Levi's *The Drowned and the Saved*, Ozick places in front of us Levi's shadow text. Levi, she concludes, who felt he was "a man somehow set apart from retaliatory passion," must have suddenly awakened to the fact that his rage was dormant. "I grieve," she says, "that he equated rage—the rage that speaks for mercifulness—with self-destruction." Ozick has offered the reader another light by which to read Levi's story.

This is what I mean by Ozick's intelligence, an intelligence that shone so clearly on our first meeting. She does not try to replace the reader's relationship with a book, or colour the reader's emotions. Her task (and in this she succeeds admirably) is to put to new uses the text's own metaphors, to enlarge meanings, to shine light from other angles, to test for reverberations and echoes. After Ozick's review, Levi's book is not only a testimony on Auschwitz, but an interrogation on the quest for truth, on the value of aggression, on the sense of revenge, on solutions that reveal more about the quest itself than on the trivial matter of success or failure.

This is something to which we, in our time, have grown accustomed but upon which we don't seem to have reflected sufficiently. In our stories, the hero seldom reaches his goal. The test itself is the hero's epic, independent of the often unhappy conclusion. Failure, these days, seems truer to life than success.

The chronicle of one such life is the ostensible theme of Ozick's novel *The Cannibal Galaxy*. The hero is Joseph Brill, a schoolmaster. We meet him at the age of fifty-eight, the principal of the Edmond Fleg Primary School, which he has founded somewhere in the United States. We are led back through his life to his childhood in Paris, where his fishmonger father seemed more sympathetic than his somewhat distracted mother to young Brill's love of literature, being able to delight "in the iridescent scales of an ordinary *morue*." We are made witnesses to the boy's escapades into culture—the Musée Carnavalet, a trip to London and a meeting with an old E. M. Forster–like writer. Finally, the war: Brill escapes the Nazi roundups and is hidden by nuns in a cellar while, unheard by him (but we, the readers, know more), his youngest sister screams throughout the infernal day in the Vel'd'Hiv. After the war, he comes to America and founds a school. Then the novel begins.

Ozick's biographical intent is made clear in two epigraphs —one by Yehuda Amichai, asking where his place might be between the two well-matched halves of this world, those who love and those who hate, and another by Emily Dickinson: "The Rest of Life to See!/ Past Midnight! Past the Morning Star!" Yet Brill's biography is only the apparent subject. Throughout, like the scarlet undercoat the Dutch painters applied to their canvases, a fiercer story shines through: a story of devoured galaxies, engulfed traditions, changing generations and lost souls. Brill's life becomes a vantage point from which Ozick shows us an epic fresco, ageless and endless. And because the author is Cynthia Ozick, the epic is, of course, the history of the Jews.

Brill is one of the many faces of the surviving Jew, a man who tries to compromise and fails, not because his task is doomed by fate (fatalism would be "contrary to our teaching," says Brill) but because his task is impossible. Compromise, the middle way, leads nowhere. And Brill is essentially a creature of compromise.

Brill chooses for his school a dual curriculum that combines the Jewish and French traditions; he sets it up in Middle America, in the centre of a lake, "as though he had a horror of coasts and margins, of edges and extremes of any sort." On this island, Brill never succeeds in holding his students' interest, nor does he recognize genius when it comes his way. When the famous "imagistic linguistic logician" Hester Lift enrols her daughter Beulah, Brill, Lear-like, dismisses the subdued child. Instead, he places all his hopes on his son, who ends up studying business administration in Miami.

And yet, even along his chosen middle road, Brill is pushed onward by a vital thrust: the urge to survive. Not simply being, but growing, increasing, while threatened as a Jew by the cannibal galaxy of Christian culture. Survival, in Brill's case, is achieved by assimilation—a reverse assimilation, taking the outside world and making it his own, cannibalizing the cannibal.

The astonishing discovery that Ozick helps us make is that survival can be, at its best, a secret event: not even the survivor needs to be aware of it. Brill's son finds his own commercial way; Hester Lift triumphs in her own terms; Beulah fulfils her promise; even the failed Brill succeeds, however unwittingly, because his school brings about Beulah's success. Even though we choose to forget it, or deny it, or pretend to ignore it (Ozick argues) God is generous. Perhaps her books are largely about the generosity of God.

In his introduction to Herbert Read's masterpiece, *The Green Child*, Graham Greene says that art is always the resolution of a combat. But is this always the case? Surely sometimes it is the combat itself that, unresolved, becomes a work of art, offering no outcome, waiting, hoping against hope, for the Messiah of its resolution. The description of this combat, during which the writer doesn't answer but asks questions, unfolding possibilities and resolving nothing, is in many cases, I believe, more satisfying than the literature of outcome, which often smacks of moral fable.

All of Ozick's fiction shares this unfolding quality. In *The Messiah of Stockholm*, for instance, Ozick invents the story of a man who invents his story—his name, his birth, his ancestry—reshaping his daily life to make it unreal to others but real to himself. For Lars Andemening, the outside world is a person from Porlock. Lars, like Coleridge, is a dreamer.

He is also a book reviewer for a small Swedish newspaper. He never knew his parents—he is an orphan smuggled into Sweden during the Nazi terror—but he has convinced himself that his father was the great Polish writer Bruno Schulz, murdered by the SS in 1942. Lars has no proof of this parentage except his own conviction, which has made him a half-hearted misanthrope. His only confidante is a German bookseller named Heidi, a woman protected from both affection and pain by a cocoon of scorn. Heidi provides Lars first with a teacher of Polish, then with Polish books to learn the language of his chosen father.

Schulz's entire oeuvre consists of two volumes, *Sanatorium under the Sign of the Hourglass* and *The Street of Crocodiles*, plus a few letters and drawings. Missing is a novel scholars suppose to have been Schulz's masterpiece, *The Messiah*.

One day, Heidi tells Lars that a woman calling herself Adela (the name of a character in Schulz's books) has appeared out of the blue with the lost manuscript in a plastic bag; she says she is Schulz's daughter. According to Heidi and her husband, Dr. Eklund, *The Messiah* has returned. Lars's reality, and therefore his sanity, is threatened. "There's no room in the story for another child," he says to Heidi. "It's not feasible. It can't be." For Lars's story to make dramatic sense, there must be only one child, Lars himself. Adela must therefore be a fraud, and *The Messiah*, the long-awaited, much thirsted-for *Messiah*, must be a false one.

The choice of Schulz as Lars's father is not fortuitous: Schulz's work is inhabited, even possessed, by the figure of the Father, a man who does not believe that Creation is exclusively the prerogative of God. In a quotation Ozick places at the beginning of her book, Schulz's Father says: "There is no dead matter ... lifelessness is only a disguise behind which hide unknown forms of life ... even if the classical methods of creation should prove inaccessible for evermore, there still remain some illegal methods, an infinity of heretical and criminal methods."

Ozick the citizen, the Jew, must have watched in awe as Ozick the writer, the pagan, rolled out her heretical chain of linked creations in Lars's story.

It is as if Lars stood between two mirrors. First, there is Ozick, who creates Lars, attributing him to "an indifferent maker" whose hand "had smeared his mouth and chin and Adam's apple." Then comes Lars himself, a reviewer, a creator, though admittedly a second-hand one. Reviewers (such as myself) are envious readers who believe in surrogate parenthood, creating texts from someone else's seed; Lars, after devouring a book he must review, falls asleep feeling "oddly fat," as if pregnant with the words the writer has created. After his sleep, he can produce his piece almost in one draft. Lars is also the creator of his own name (in secret he calls himself Lazarus Baruch), of his own time (living much by night and sleeping in the afternoon, wringing two days out of one by dividing the day in two with a nap), of his own ancestry. In third place are Heidi and Dr. Eklund, who create around Lars's world a meaner, tawdrier reality. Finally, somewhere along this line of creator-creations is God.

God provides the contrast. In the seventeenth century, Judah Loew ben Bezabel, rabbi of Prague, made an artificial man, a golem who could, it was said, do a few menial tasks around the synagogue, like sweeping the floor and ringing the bells. But something was lacking in the golem. In the eyes of those who marvelled at it, the creature was more like a thing than a person. In the end, out of pity or terror, its creator destroyed it.

Lars's reality is like the golem: to Lars it may seem more real than real life, but it lacks the iron-clad immanence of a reality made by God. Lars knows this and refuses to see the last surviving person who had been part of Schulz's life: Jozefina, Schulz's fiancée, now living in London. Lars will not see her because his reality is far too fragile to bear confrontation. Schulz himself declared (as both Lars and Heidi quote) that "reality is as thin as paper and betrays with all its cracks its imitative character." Lars, like God, will admit no other reality than his own. "He's a priest of the original," Heidi says of him. "What he wants is the original of things."

Lars accuses the Eklunds of wanting to be "in competition with God," not realizing (or realizing only vaguely) that he is guilty of that very sin. Lars also sins by imagining that God requires our belief in order to exist. Discussing the need to inform the world of the appearance of *The Messiah*, Heidi insists, "People have to be *told* it exists." And then, "If it's not believed in, it might as well not exist." "That sounds like God," is Lars's blasphemous answer.

There are books designed to have no end: they are fathomless, they have the richness of unresolved mysteries. Every time we read through them and believe we have answered all their questions, new questions arise, and then more questions. *The Messiah of Stockholm* is one such book. In part, this endless reading can be attributed to Ozick's Talmudic tradition of leaving no word idle, of pursuing each meaning to the marrow, as if the author (and the reader) were convinced that the entire Creation, including novels, was infinitely pregnant with revelation.

But there is more. When, at the end of the book, Lars comes face to face with his grief, as his phantom father vanishes "inside the narrow hallway of his skull" clutching the never-to-be-seen-again *Messiah*, we know that Lars's dream world has been shattered, and we mourn for his loss—but we are also left with a curious sense of wonder. Because in spite of murdered writers and orphaned men, Ozick realistically shows us, somewhere between bewilderment and belief, the possible beauty of the universe.

Waiting for an Echo:
On Reading Richard Outram

Writing a book of poetry is like dropping
a rose petal down the Grand Canyon
and waiting for an echo.

DON MARQUIS

1. *The Canyon*

WE ARE WHAT WE READ, but we are equally what we don't read. What we, as a society, leave on the shelves defines us at least as much as the books we gobble up. Nineteenth-century Americans are mirrored in their choice of Longfellow as their parlour poet—nationalistic, traditional, hardly ever uncomfortable. But they are also mirrored by their misunderstanding, if not rejection, of Herman Melville—universalist, difficult and very unconventional.

Until the 1960s, Canada barely acknowledged the existence of Canadian literature. When, thanks to the perseverance of young writers such as Margaret Atwood, and stubborn editors such as Robert Weaver, Canadian readers made the discovery that this literature existed, the pantheon of writers chosen to represent it set a style against which the writing to come was measured. The most vociferous representatives of the newly discovered literature were poets, and small publishers of poetry—Anansi, Talonbooks, Coach House Press—were among its most energetic champions. In very broad terms, the style of what became recognized as Canadian poetry was simple-sounding, chatty, intimate but never overwhelmingly passionate, well-mannered though sometimes effectively ironic, often funny, in obligatory free verse. Leafing through what may well be one of the pantheon's canonical books, the *New Oxford Book of Canadian Verse*, edited by Atwood (though published in 1982, it still echoes the sixties' tenets) one is struck by the overall lightness of its tone and vocabulary, even in poets as seemingly dissimilar as Irving Layton and Paulette Jiles.

A few lines, chosen at random, will illustrate what I mean: "my love is young & i am old/ she'll need a new man soon" (Earle Birney); "A soldier is a man who is not a man" (Eli Mandel); "I live like a trapeze artist with a headache, my poems are no aspirins" (Milton Acorn); "Though what would a god be *like*—would he shop at Dominion?" (Dennis Lee). It is as if, in the long beginning, Canadian literature chose to be easy. This, perhaps, explains why certain poets, Atwood included, are remembered for their lighter verse, and others whose work seems more complex are virtually ignored. Among those notable for their absence from the Canadian pantheon is one of the finest poets in the English language: Richard Outram.

My acquaintance with Outram's work dates from 1979, when the publisher Louise Dennys, exercising that prerogative of friendship which consists in forcing books upon a friend, suggested that I read a slim volume called *Turns*. On page 40 was a poem that had almost all the characteristics of Canadian poetry listed earlier, and yet was something different, profound.

Bearded Lady

I am in fact a public slave;
How I would like to misbehave
And start the morning with a shave;

But do not dare. Each day I rise
To face my face with downcast eyes
And make the toilette I despise,

So that, my moustache all unfurled,
My whiskers neatly oiled and curled,
I may go forth to face the world.

To bear all day the cruellest whips
Of dirty jokes and jeers and quips;
I am adept at reading lips.

Hell hath indeed, as we are warned,
No fury like a woman scorned:
God knows why I am so adorned.

He may not find, for all His Grace,
A member of the human race
To love me for my hirsute face;

But when the world and time have died
You'll face me, seated by His side,
His radiant and bearded Bride.

I was overwhelmed by the intelligence, passion, and music of this concise collection, and by the robust joyfulness that echoed the ancient Talmudic warning: "A man is to give account in the Hereafter for any permissible pleasures from which he abstained." Lines stayed with me, bred ideas, gave sense to experience. When later I needed an epigraph for an anthology of fantastic literature I was editing, two couplets read in *Turns* spelled out the essence of what I was trying to say:

> From one who maintains, there is nothing beyond
> The Human Imagination; or another
>
> Soul who contends, by night, that beyond
> The human imagination, there is Nothing?

Turns made me want to read more of Outram's work. I soon found that bookstores assiduously ignored him, and that he was absent from the libraries of most of my friends. I discovered, in fact, that Outram's entire career had been one of absences. He has never received a national, let alone international award, or a Canada Council grant; he has never been included in any major anthology of Canadian poetry, rarely been acknowledged in reviews. Perhaps there is a reason for the silence surrounding Outram's work. At work in his poems is that creature derided in so much of our accepted literature: that most unpopular of citizens, the moralist, the person who, in the simplest terms, is concerned with how we behave in the world.

After reading Outram, I wanted to meet him. This was in 1979. Since then, several years of conversations have shown me that he is not concerned with picture postcards of heaven and hell: his interest is in conduct, not in punishments and rewards; in our reactions to the everyday flow, in how, by everything we do, we affect ourselves and the world around us.

Outram was born in Oshawa, Ontario, in 1930 and graduated from Victoria College, University of Toronto. From 1956 to 1990, he worked as a stage hand at the CBC. With his wife, the artist Barbara Howard, he founded in 1960 the Gauntlet Press, where he printed several sequences of his poems later collected in other volumes. His first book, *Eight Poems*, was published by the Tortoise Press in 1959—the press's single production. A few years later, an editor at Macmillan Canada invited him to submit a manuscript. The result was *Exultate, Jubilate*, published in 1966. Macmillan, however, rejected Outram's next collection, as did several other publishers. Louise Dennys, who had just resigned as an editor at Clarke Irwin, was outraged at the rejection and took Outram's manuscript with her to England, where she convinced Chatto & Windus to publish it in their prestigious *Phoenix* series. Chatto agreed, on condition that a Canadian publisher be recruited to help with the production costs.

Outram found a co-publisher in a Toronto antiquarian bookseller, Hugh Anson-Cartwright, who, joining forces with Dennys, created Anson-Cartwright Editions in 1975 and published *Turns*. Anson-Cartwright also published Outram's next book, *The Promise of Light*, in a limited edition of 250 copies. As it turned out, Outram was not the only author in the new press's catalogue; in 1978 it published another obscure Canadian, the Czech émigré novelist Josef Skvorecky, later nominated for the Nobel Prize.

Since the publication of *Turns*, Outram's work has appeared under two other imprints. In 1985 his *Selected Poems* was published by Exile Editions and, a year later, *Man in Love* was published by Porcupine's Quill, which also published Outram's following books: *Hiram and Jenny* in 1988 and *Mogul Recollected* in 1993.

2. *The Echo*

Hiram and Jenny is a good starting-place. At its core are man and woman, that multitudinous couple, sitting at the water's edge and leading lives that, like those of Adam and Eve, contain the whole of mankind—every thought, every war, every discovery, every death to come. "Every man," Ralph Waldo Emerson wrote with moving conviction, "is an inlet to the same and to all of the same ... what at any time has fallen to any man he can understand." Hiram and Jenny exercise that understanding.

They are common folk. Hiram has his banjo and his bodily aches; Jenny her neighbours and her newspaper. They go to movies at the Palace and to slide shows at the church. But Hiram and Jenny are also gods and heroes: Hiram becomes Icarus at the fall fair, plunging from a "slicker-yellow biplane" which he rides for $5.50. Jenny sees Jehovah in a moth caught on fire. Jenny metamorphoses into the four primordial elements. A seal offers Hiram Poseidon's throne.

> ... Hiram shuddered, knowing the cold's
> bone stealth, the crushed lightless abysm.
> Said, "No!"

History's greats visit them. A snake becomes Diogenes the Cynic to Jenny's Alexander, asking her to "step aside, / stop blocking the sun." Plato comes to visit and he and Hiram go fishing. Beethoven talks to Hiram about the afterlife. A monarch butterfly turns out to be the Apostle Paul. Episode after episode, poem after poem, Outram builds a cosmology of sorts, rethinking our relationship to everyone and everything, writing, as Gosse said of Kipling, "with the whole of the English language" and the whole of humankind's events.

One of the most memorable poems in the volume is "Techne." Here is Hiram crouched, washing his socks in a creek, while

> Not far offshore, unseen,
> crammed with warheads and comic books,
> a nuclear submarine
> noses about with her cornfed crew

The submarine "buggers off"; Hiram continues to wash his socks, one yellow, one green with orange stripes.

> ... No doubt
> God's socks match in mysterious ways.
> Washed in the Blood of the Lamb,
> The Dead shall rise up on the Last Day.
> Hiram don't give a damn.

Hiram's conduct, his concern with immediate responsibilities, the awful and ludicrous importance of his assigned task, becomes suddenly clear. Comprehension follows surprise, compassion replaces curiosity. Hiram and Jenny's God is like the gods of Greece and Rome, prone to human weaknesses that do not diminish His divinity, but illuminate instead man and woman's Godlike essence promised (or revealed) in the Garden. Outram humanizes God's mysteries, picturing man's plight and God's tremendous covenant—why not?—as the washing of socks.

If one poem in *Hiram and Jenny* could sum up Outram's credo, that poem would be "Error," in which both heroes bring light into water by entering it themselves.

Hiram's discovered desire is to enter water
as light enters water and alters it not,
yet sets quick fire beneath the surface,
as rapture may enter a body held in thought;

even as water remains the reflecting semblance
that turns burning, that casts back shattered fire
manyfold into the blinded beholder's eye,
to enter water discovered is Hiram's desire;

even as cold motionless depths unsounded
by light or the lost rumour of light remain
haven of absent creatures, beings we deem
monstrous for light stricken from their domain;

yet into this radiant world Hiram and Jenny
slip together, bright in each other's sight,
as a vessel, surging, divides the featureless waters
that cleft, curled, breaking, may enter light.

"Error" recognizes the paradoxical quality of everyday experience, how the simplest things—water, light—mirror endless streams of meaning, which we who take part in the experience, who merely read it, transform by our presence. By the elemental act of bathing, with all its sexual reverberations, Outram's man and woman become the God of Creation who changed, the Book of Genesis tells us, "the darkness upon the face of the deep."

Our divine quality does not, however, make us any wiser, as Outram's next book, *Mogul Recollected*, suggests. Outram's long elegy for Mogul, an elephant drowned during a New Brunswick ferry crossing in 1836, ends like this:

Being not man nor angel but beast, Mogul
saw not through his eye but with it life
in the myriad present: which is immortal.

And he beheld, as he was beholden to,
what he became: his one death.

After *Mogul*, Outram began a series of visionary poems. His sybil is Ms. Cassie, sister of Yeats's Crazy Jane, what, in another context, Outram calls one of the "Prophets of mundane doom." Ms. Cassie speaks with Death and with the sun, reads palms and the Bible, suffers second sight. True seer, she sees the paradox of the obvious: "a cross/ nailed to a man," "Eve, released by design/ from his rib-/ cage," that "Given its blind due the dead/ moon will rise. . . ." These paradoxes are our daily reality.

"Things thought too long can be no longer thought," wrote Yeats in 1936, in one of his last poems. Ms. Cassie echoes this adamantine law (in "Ms. Cassie Writes an Open Letter"):

Death at first
it is borne in upon us
it is immortal delight it is past
our understanding it was ever thus.

Now for the last time may we be made aware.

That nothing and nothing went wrong.
It is never a question of belief.
It is the harrowed lifelong
brevity of grief.

Long thought has wasted fear of death to the bone, down to a "lifelong brevity of grief," but between the lines of Ms. Cassie's letter lurks a multiplicity of ancient notions. A stoic truism: "Death: at first it is borne in upon us. It is immortal delight. It is past our understanding. It was ever thus." An Augustinian hope: "Death at first. It is borne. In, upon, us, it is immortal delight. It is past. Our understanding: it was ever thus." A Lutheran conviction: "Death: at first it is borne in upon us. It is immortal. Delight: it is past our understanding. It was ever thus." All these readings are possible, none is definitive, every one is implied. In Ms. Cassie's poems Outram has achieved what Yeats expected from a "truthful poem": "I had in my memory," wrote Yeats in a note appended in 1933 to *The Winding Stair*, "Byzantine mosaic pictures of the Annunciation, which show a line drawn from a star to the ear of the Virgin. She received the Word through the ear, a star fell, and a star was born." These simultaneous revelations co-exist in Outram's poems.

Each new writer who, in the eyes of even one reader, becomes essential to understanding the world, changes history, provides a new order, demands a new reading of the past. Outram restores to our poetry a brash intimacy with metaphysics that has become somehow unacceptable in our time. Outram's predecessors are among the seventeenth-century English poets, George Herbert in particular, John Donne of course, and two major American poets, Emily Dickinson and Wallace Stevens. Reading Outram suggests that these previously unrelated writers have, in fact, common bonds, which Outram has brought to light: a happy kinship with the holy.

"Poets in our civilization," said Eliot, "must be difficult." Our tired times, however, have led us to avoid the difficult or, worse, to regard it as ostentatious and pedantic. We are asked to accept this paradox: that what is profound is superfluous. This has become our excuse for being lazy. Of course, at all times readers have had silly rules dictating their fashion in literature. The canonical book of Victorian poetry, Palgrave's *Golden Treasury*, excluded Donne and most of the metaphysical poets who weren't considered "accomplished"; it wasn't until Oscar Williams revised the *Treasury* in 1953 that redress was made.

Readers mature later than writers and require certain mysterious preparations to receive them properly. Fortunately, good writing is persistent. It will not go away. It is there to translate much of our dealing with the world and with ourselves, to give voice to our questions. It isn't easy, in the sense that language itself isn't easy, but it is clear and resonant. We, of course, have no obligation to listen to its echo. As usual, we have the choice of remaining deaf.

IX

GETTING RID OF THE ARTISTS

"And what does *it* live on?"

"Weak tea with cream in it."

A new difficulty came into Alice's head. "Supposing it couldn't find any?" she suggested.

"Then it would die, of course."

"But that must happen very often," Alice remarked thoughtfully.

"It always happens," said the Gnat.

Through the Looking-Glass, Chapter III

Jonah and the Whale

A Sermon

in memory of Paul Fleck

"Oh, Time, Strength, Cash, and Patience!"

HERMAN MELVILLE,
Moby-Dick, Chapter XXXII

Of all the snarling or moaning prophets who haunt the pages of the Old Testament, I believe that none is so curious as the prophet known as Jonah. I like Jonah. I have a fondness for Jonah, in spite of his posthumous reputation as a purveyor of bad luck. I think I've discovered what it was about Jonah that made people nervous in his presence. I think Jonah had what in the nineteenth century was called an artistic temperament. I think Jonah was an artist.

The first time I heard the story of Jonah, it was from a great-uncle of mine, who had the disagreeable habit of spitting into his handkerchief when he talked. He had a small claim to Jewish scholarship, which we believed did not go far beyond the few verses he taught us to memorize for our bar mitzvah. But sometimes he could tell a good story, and if you didn't look too closely at the spittle forming at the corners of his mouth, the experience could be quite entertaining. The story of Jonah came about one day when I was being especially pigheaded, refusing to do something or other I had been asked to do for the one-hundredth time. "Just like Jonah," said my great-uncle, holding his handkerchief to his mouth, spitting heartily and tucking the handkerchief deep into his pocket. "Always no, no, no. What will you grow up to be? An anarchist?" For my great-uncle, who in spite of the pogroms had always felt an curious admiration for the tsar, there was nothing worse than an anarchist, except perhaps a journalist. He said that journalists were all peeping Toms and Nosy Parkers, and that if you wanted to find out what was going on in the world you could do so from your friends in the café. Which he did, day in, day out, except, of course, on the Shabbath.

The story of Jonah was probably written sometime in the fourth or fifth century B.C. The Book of Jonah is one of the shortest in the Bible—and one of the strangest. It tells how the prophet Jonah was summoned by God to go and cry against the city of Nineveh, whose wickedness had reached the ears of Heaven. But Jonah refused, because he knew that through his word the Ninevites would repent and God would forgive them. To escape the divine order, Jonah jumped on a ship sailing for Tarshish. A furious storm rose, the sailors moaned in despair and Jonah, somehow understanding that he was the cause of this meteorological turmoil, asked to be thrown into the sea to calm the waves. The sailors obliged, the storm died down, and Jonah was swallowed by a great fish, appointed for this purpose by God Himself. There in the bowels of the fish Jonah remained for three long days and three long nights. On the fourth day, the Lord caused the great fish to vomit the prophet out onto dry land and, once again, the Lord ordered Jonah to go to Nineveh and speak to the people. This time Jonah obeyed. The King of Nineveh heard the warning, immediately repented, and the city of Nineveh was saved. But Jonah was furious with the Lord and stormed out into the desert to the east of the city, where he set up a sort of booth and sat and waited to see what would become of the repentant Nineveh. The Lord then caused a plant to sprout up and protect Jonah from the sun. Jonah expressed his gratitude for the divine gift, but next morning, the Lord caused the plant to wither. The sun and the wind beat hard on Jonah, and faint with heat he told the Lord it was better for him to die. Then the Lord spoke to Jonah and said: "You are upset because I killed a simple plant and yet you wished me to destroy all the people of Nineveh. Should I have spared a plant but not spared these people 'who do not know their right hand from their left,' *and* also much cattle?" With this unanswered question, the Book of Jonah ends.

I am fascinated by the reason for Jonah's refusal to prophesy in Nineveh. The idea that Jonah would keep away from performing his divinely inspired piece *because* he knew his audience would repent and be therefore forgiven, must seem incomprehensible to anyone except an artist. Jonah knew that Ninevite society dealt in one of two ways with its artists: either it saw the accusation in an artist's work and blamed the artist for the evils of which the society stood accused, or it assimilated the artist's work because, valued in dinars and nicely framed, the art could serve as a pleasant decoration. In such circumstances, Jonah knew, no artist can win.

Given the choice between creating an accusation or a decoration, Jonah would have probably preferred the accusation. Like most artists, what Jonah really wanted was to stir the languid hearts of his listeners, to touch them, to awaken in them something vaguely known and yet utterly mysterious, to trouble their dreams and to haunt their waking hours. What he certainly did not want, under any circumstances, was their repentance. Having the listeners simply say to themselves, "All's forgiven and forgotten, let's bury the past, let's not talk about injustice and the need for retribution, cuts in education and health programs, unequal taxation and unemployment; let exploiters shake hands with exploited, and on to our next glorious money-making hour"—no, that was something Jonah certainly did not want. Nadine Gordimer, of whom Jonah had never heard, said that there could be no worse fate for a writer than *not* being execrated in a corrupt society. Jonah did not wish to suffer that annihilating fate.

Above all, Jonah was aware of Nineveh's ongoing war between the politicians and the artists, a war in which Jonah felt that all the artists' efforts (beyond the efforts demanded by their craft) were ultimately futile because they took place in the political arena. It was a well-known fact that Ninevite artists (who had never tired in the pursuit of their own art) grew quickly weary of the struggle with bureaucrats and banks, and the few heroes who had continued the fight against the corrupt secretaries of state and royal lackeys had done so many times at the expense of both their art and their sanity. It was very difficult to go to your studio or to your clay tablets after a day of committee meetings. The bureaucrats of Nineveh counted on this, of course, and one of their most effective tactics was delay: delaying agreements, delaying the attribution of funds, delaying contracts, delaying appointments, delaying outright answers. If you waited long enough, they said, the rage of the artist would fade, or rather mysteriously turn into creative energy: the artist would go away and write a poem or do an installation or dream up a dance. And these things represented little danger to banks and private corporations. In fact, as business people well knew, many times this artistic rage became marketable merchandise. "Think," the Ninevites often said, "how much you'd pay today for the work of painters who in their time hardly had enough money to buy paint, let alone food. For an artist," they added knowingly, "posthumous fame is its own reward."

But the great triumph of Ninevite politicians was their success in getting the artists to work against themselves. So imbued was Nineveh with the idea that wealth was the city's goal, and that art, since it was not an immediate producer of wealth, was an undeserving pursuit, that the artists themselves came to believe that they should pay their own way in the world, producing cost-efficient art, frowning on failure and lack of recognition, and above all, trying to gratify those who, being wealthy, were also in positions of power. So visual artists were asked to make their work more pleasing, composers to write music with a hummable tune, writers to imagine not-so-depressing scenarios, since, in the words of Dorothy Parker (who as far as I know was not from Nineveh):

Oh, life is a glorious cycle of song
A medley of extemporanea,
And love is a thing that can never go wrong
And I am Marie of Roumania.

In times long gone by, in short periods during which the bureaucrats slumbered, certain funds had been granted to artistic causes by soft-hearted or soft-headed Ninevite kings. Since those times, more conscientious officials had been redressing this financial oversight and vigorously pruning down the allotted sums. No official would, of course, recognize any such change in the government's support of the arts, and yet the Ninevite secretary of finance was able to cut the actual funds allotted to the arts down to almost nothing, while at the same time advertising a committed increase of those same funds in the official records. This was done by the use of certain devices borrowed from the Ninevite poets (whose tools the politicians happily pilfered, while despising the poets who invented them). Metonymy, for instance, the device by which a poet uses a part or an attribute of something to stand in its place ("crown" for "king" for example), allowed the secretary of provisions to cut down on the funds spent on subsidizing artists' work materials. All any artist now received from the City, whatever his needs, was a number-four rat-hair paintbrush, since in the secretary's official vocabulary "brush" was made to stand for "the ensemble of an artist's equipment." Metaphors, the most common of poetic tools, were employed to great effect by these financial wizards. In one celebrated case, a sum of ten thousand gold dinars had been set aside long ago for the lodging of senior artists. By simply redefining camels, used in public transport, as "temporary lodgings," the secretary of finance was able to count the cost of the camels' upkeep (for which the City of Nineveh was responsible) as part of the sum allotted to artists' lodgings, since the senior artists did indeed use subsidized public camels to get from place to place.

"The real artists," said the Ninevites, "have no cause to complain. If they are really good at what they do, they will make a buck no matter what the social conditions. It's the others, the so-called experimenters, the self-indulgers, the prophets, who don't make a cent and whine about their condition. A banker who doesn't know how to turn a profit would be equally lost. A bureaucrat who didn't recognize the need to clog things down would be out of a job. This is the law of survival. Nineveh is a society that looks to the future."

True: in Nineveh, a handful of artists (and many con artists) made a good living. Ninevite society liked to reward a few of the makers of the products it consumed. What it would not recognize, of course, was the vast majority of the artists whose attempts and glitterings and failures allowed the successes of others to be born. Ninevite society didn't have to support anything it didn't instantly like or understand. The truth was that this vast majority of artists would carry on, of course, no matter what, simply because they couldn't help it, the Lord or the Holy Spirit urging them on night after night. They carried on writing and painting and composing and dancing by whatever means they could find. "Like every other worker in society," the Ninevites said.

It is told that the first time Jonah heard this particular point of Ninevite wisdom, he drummed up his prophetic courage and stood in the public square of Nineveh to address the crowds. "The artist," Jonah attempted to explain, "is *not* like every other worker in society. The artist deals with reality: inner and outer reality transformed into meaningful symbols. Those who deal in money deal in symbols behind which stands nothing. It is wonderful to think of the thousands and thousands of Ninevite stockbrokers for whom reality, the real world, is the arbitrary rising and falling of figures transformed in their imagination into wealth—a wealth that exists only on a piece of paper or on a flickering screen. No fantasy writer, no virtual reality artist could ever aspire to create in an audience such an all-pervading suspension of disbelief as that which takes place in an assembly of stockbrokers. Grown-up men and women who will not for a minute consider the reality of the unicorn, even as a symbol, will accept as rock-hard fact that they possess a share in the nation's camel bellies, and in that belief they consider themselves happy and secure."

By the time Jonah had reached the end of this paragraph, the public square of Nineveh was deserted.

For all these reasons, Jonah decided to escape both Nineveh and the Lord, and jumped on a ship headed for Tarshish.

Now, the sailors in the ship that carried Jonah were all men from Joppa, a port not far from Nineveh, an outpost of the Ninevite empire. Nineveh was, as you have no doubt surmised, a society besotted by greed. Not ambition, which is a creative impulse, something all artists possess, but the sterile impulse to accumulate for the sake of accumulation. Joppa, however, had for many decades been a place where prophets had been allowed a tolerable amount of freedom. The people of Joppa accepted the yearly influx of bearded, ragged men and dishevelled, wild-eyed women with a certain degree of sympathy, since their presence procured Joppa free publicity when the prophets travelled abroad to other cities, where they often mentioned the name of Joppa in not unkind terms. Also, the recurrent prophesying season brought curious and illustrious visitors to Joppa, and neither the innkeepers nor the owners of the caravanserais complained of the demands made on their bed and board.

But when times were hard in Nineveh and the economic hardships of the city rippled out all the way to the little town of Joppa, when business profits were up only a mere 74 per cent and the wealthy Joppites were constrained to sell one of their ornamented six-horse chariots, or close down a couple of their upland sweatshops, then the presence in Joppa of the prophesying artists was openly frowned upon. The tolerance and whimsical generosity of wealthier days seemed now sinfully wasteful to the citizens of Joppa, and many of them felt that the artists who came to their quaint little haven should make no demands at all and feel grateful for whatever they got: grateful when they were lodged in the frumpiest buildings of Joppa, grateful when they were denied appropriate working tools, grateful when they had funds cut for new projects. When they were forced to move out of their rooms to accommodate paying guests from Babylon, the artists were told to remember that they, as artists, should know that it was an honourable thing to lie under the stars wrapped in smelly goat hides just like the illustrious prophets and poets of the days before the Flood. Above all, they were told to dismiss their elitist ideas: such as the notion that artists need to be among artists in order to exchange ideas, discuss craft, collaborate and learn, or that they should be free to move about dressed however they liked, and do whatever they wanted, without having a visiting Babylonian conference participant stare at them in amusement or disgust.

And yet even during those difficult times, most Joppites retained for the prophets a certain sincere fondness, somewhat akin to the affection we feel for old pets who have been around since our childhood, and they tried in several ways to accommodate them even when the going was not good, and attempted not to hurt their artistic sensibilities by being too blunt in their dealings. Thus it was that when the storm rose and the ship from Joppa was tossed by furious waves, the Joppite sailors felt uneasy, and hesitated before blaming Jonah, their artistic guest. Unwilling to take any drastic measures, they tried praying to their own gods, who they knew commanded the heavens and the seas—but with no visible results. In fact, the storm only got worse, as if the Joppite gods had other things to think about and were annoyed by the sailors' whiny requests. Then the sailors appealed to Jonah (who was in the hold, sleeping out the storm, as artists sometimes do), and woke him and asked him for advice. Even when Jonah told them, with a touch of artistic pride, that the storm was all his fault, the sailors felt reluctant to toss him overboard. How much of a gale could one scraggy artist raise? How angry could one miserable prophet make the deep, wine-dark sea? But the storm grew worse, the wind howled through the riggings, the planks groaned and cried out when the waves hit them, and in the end, one by one, the sailors remembered the old Ninevite truisms, learned in Joppa at their grandmother's knee: that all artists were, by and large, freeloaders, and that all Jonah and his type did all day was compose poems in which they kvetched about this and moaned about that, and said threatening things about the most innocent vices. And why should a society in which greed is the driving force support someone who does not contribute in the least to the immediate accumulation of wealth? Therefore, as one of the sailors explained to his mates, don't blame yourselves for bad seamanship, simply accept Jonah's *mea culpa*, and throw the bastard into the water. He won't resist. In fact, he just about asked for it.

Now, even if Jonah had had second thoughts, and had argued that perhaps a ship, or a ship of state, could in fact do with a few wise prophecies to serve as ballast and keep it steady, the sailors had learned from long familiarity with Ninevite politicians the craft of turning a deaf ear to artistic warnings. Zigzagging their way across the oceans of the world in search of new lands on which to conduct free and profitable trade, the sailors assumed that whatever an artist might say or do, the weight of money would always provide a steadier ballast than any artistic argument.

When they threw Jonah overboard and the sea became calm again, the sailors fell on their knees and thanked the Lord, the God of Jonah. No one enjoys being tossed about in a rocking boat, and since the rocking had stopped as soon as Jonah hit the water, the sailors immediately concluded that he was indeed to blame and that their action had been fully justified. These sailors had obviously not had the benefit of a classical education, or they would have known that the argument for the elimination of the artist was to acquire in the centuries to come a long and venerable history. They would have known that there is an ancient impulse, running through the very foundations of every human society, to shun that uncomfortable creature who keeps attempting to shift the tenets of our certitudes, the rock on which we like to believe we stand. For Plato, to begin with, the real artist is the statesman, the person who shapes the state according to a divine model of Justice and Beauty. The ordinary artist, on the other hand, the writer or the painter, does not reflect this worthy reality but produces instead mere fantasies, which are unfit for the education of the people. This notion, that art is only useful if it serves the state, was heartily embraced by successions of diverse governments: the Emperor Augustus banished the poet Ovid because of something the poet had written and which Augustus felt was secretly threatening. The Church condemned artists who distracted the faithful from the dogma. In the Renaissance, artists were bought and sold like courtesans and in the eighteenth century they were reduced (at least in the public imagination) to garret-living creatures dying of melancholy and consumption. Flaubert defined the nineteenth-century bourgeois view of the artist in his *Dictionary of Clichés*: "Artists: All clowns. Praise their selflessness. Be astonished at the fact they dress like everyone else. They earn fabulous sums but they squander every last cent. Often invited to dinner at the best houses. All female artists are sluts." In our time, the descendants of the Joppite sailors have issued a *fatwa* against Salman Rushdie and hanged Ken Saro-Wiwa in Nigeria. Their motto, regarding artists, is the one coined by the Canadian immigration functionary in charge of receiving Jewish refugees during the Second World War: "None is too many."

So Jonah was thrown into the water and was swallowed by a giant fish. Life in the dark soft belly of the fish was actually not that bad. During those three days and three nights, lulled by the rumblings of ill-digested plankton and shrimp, Jonah had time to reflect. This is a luxury artists seldom have. In the belly of the fish there were no deadlines, no grocer's bills to pay, no diapers to wash, no dinners to cook, no family conflicts to be dragged into just as the right note comes to complete the sonata, no bank managers to plead with, no critics to gnash teeth over. So during those three days and three nights Jonah thought and prayed and slept and dreamed. And when he woke up, he found himself vomited onto dry land and the nagging Voice of the Lord was at him again: "Go on, go seek out Nineveh and do your bit. It doesn't matter how they react. Every artist needs an audience. You owe it to your work."

This time Jonah did as the Lord told him. Some degree of confidence in the importance of his craft had come to him in the fish's dark belly, and he felt moved to put his art on display in Nineveh. But barely had he begun his performance piece, barely had he said five words of his prophetic text, when the King of Nineveh fell on his knees and repented, the people of Nineveh ripped open their designer shirts and repented, and even the cattle of Nineveh bellowed out in unison to show that they too, repented. And the King, the people and the cattle of Nineveh all dressed in sackcloth and ashes, and assured one another that bygones were bygones, and sang Ninevite versions of "Auld Lang Syne" together, and wailed their repentance to the Lord above. And seeing this orgiastic display of repentance, the Lord withdrew his threat over the people and cattle of Nineveh. And Jonah, of course, was furious. What my great-uncle would have called the "anarchic" spirit rebelled inside Jonah, and he went off to sulk in the desert at some distance from the forgiven city.

You will remember that God had caused a plant to grow from the bare soil to shade Jonah from the heat, and that this charitable gesture of God made Jonah once again thankful, after which God withered the plant back into the dust and Jonah found himself roasting in the sun once again. We don't know whether God's trick with the plant—first placing it there to shade Jonah from the sun, and then killing it off—was a lesson meant to convince Jonah of God's good intentions. Perhaps Jonah saw in the gesture an allegory of the grants first given to him and then withdrawn after the cuts by the Nineveh Arts Council—a gesture that left him to fry unprotected in the midday sun. I suppose he understood that in times of difficulty—in times when the poor are poorer and the rich can barely keep in the million-dollar tax bracket—God wasn't going to concern Himself with questions of artistic merit. Being an Author Himself, God had no doubt some sympathy with Jonah's predicament: wanting time to work on his thoughts without having to think about his bread and butter; wanting his prophecies to appear on the *Nineveh Times* bestseller list and yet not wanting to be confused with the authors of potboilers and tearjerkers; wanting to stir the crowds with his searing words, but to stir them into revolt, not into submission; wanting Nineveh to look deep into its soul and recognize that its strength, its wisdom, its very life lay not in the piles of coins growing daily like funeral pyramids on the moneylenders' desks, but in the work of its artists and the words of its poets, and in the visionary rage of its prophets whose job it was to keep the boat rocking in order to keep the citizens awake. All this the Lord understood, as he understood Jonah's anger, because it isn't impossible to imagine that God Himself sometimes learns something from His artists.

However, though God could draw water from a stone and cause the people of Nineveh to repent, He still could not make them think. The cattle, incapable of thought, He could pity. But speaking to Jonah as Creator to creator, as Artist to artist, what was God to do with a people who, as He said with such divine irony, "don't know their right hand from their left"?

At this, I imagine, Jonah nodded, and was silent.

X

REMEMBERING THE FUTURE

"—but there's one great advantage in it, that one's memory works both ways."

Through the Looking-Glass, Chapter v

St. Augustine's Computer

> We must let the contradictions stand as what they are, make them understood as contradictions, and grasp what lies beneath them.
>
> HANNAH ARENDT,
> *Love and Saint Augustine*

IN THE FIRST YEARS OF THE sixteenth century, the elders of the guild of San Giorgio degli Schiavoni in Venice commissioned the artist Vittore Carpaccio to paint a series of scenes illustrating the life of St. Jerome, the fourth-century reader and scholar. The last scene, now set up high on the right as you enter the small and darkened guild hall, is not a portrait of St. Jerome but of St. Augustine of Hippo, St. Jerome's contemporary. In a story popular since the Middle Ages, it was told that St. Augustine had sat down at his desk to write to St. Jerome, asking his opinion on the question of eternal beatitude, when the room filled with light and Augustine heard a voice telling him that Jerome's spirit had ascended to the heavens.

The room in which Carpaccio placed Augustine is a Venetian study of Carpaccio's time, as worthy of the author of the *Confessions* as of the spirit of Jerome, responsible for the Latin version of the Bible and patron saint of translators: thin volumes face forward on a high shelf, delicate bric-à-brac lined beneath it, a brass-studded leather chair and a small writing-desk lifted from the flood-prone floor, a distant table with a rotating lectern beyond the door far left, and the Saint's working-space, cluttered with open books and with those private objects which the years wash onto every writer's desk—a seashell, a bell, a silver box. Set in the central alcove, a statue of the risen Christ looks towards a statuette of Venus standing among Augustine's things; both inhabit, admittedly on different planes, the same human world: the flesh from whose delights Augustine prayed for release ("but not just now") and the *logos*, God's Word that was in the beginning and whose echo Augustine heard one afternoon in a garden. At an obedient distance, a small, white, shaggy dog is expectantly watching.

This place depicts both the past and the present of a reader. Anachronism meant nothing to Carpaccio, since the compunction for historical faithfulness is a modern invention, not later perhaps than the nineteenth century and Ruskin's Pre-Raphaelite credo of "absolute, uncompromising truth (...) down to the most minute detail." Augustine's study and Augustine's books, whatever these might have been in the fourth century, were, to Carpaccio and his contemporaries, in all essentials much like theirs. Scrolls or codexes, bound leaves of parchment or the exquisite pocket-books that the Venetian Aldus Manutius had printed barely a few years before Carpaccio began his work at the guild, were variant forms of the book—the book that changed and would continue to change, and yet remained one and the same. In the sense in which Carpaccio saw it, Augustine's study is also like my own, a common reader's realm: the rows of books and memorabilia, the busy desk, the interrupted work, the reader waiting for a voice—his own? the author's? a spirit's?—to answer questions seeded by the open page in front of him.

Since the fellowship of readers is a generous one, or so we are told, allow me to place myself for a moment next to Carpaccio's august reader, he at his desk, I at mine. Has our reading—Augustine's and Carpaccio's and mine—altered in the passing centuries? And if so, how has it altered?

When I read a text on a page or a screen, I read silently. Through an unbelievably complex process or series of processes, clusters of neurons in specific sections of my brain decipher the text my eyes take in and make it comprehensible to me, without the need to mouth the words for the benefit of my ears. This silent reading is not as ancient a craft as we might think.

For St. Augustine, my silent activity would have been, if not incomprehensible, at the very least surprising. In a famous passage of the *Confessions*, Augustine describes his curious coming upon St. Ambrose in his cell in Milan, reading silently. "When he read," Augustine recalled, "his eyes scanned the page and his heart explored the meaning, but his voice was silent and his tongue was still." Augustine, in the fourth century, usually read as the ancient Greeks and Romans had read, out loud, to make sense of the attached strings of letters without full stops or capitals. It was possible for an experienced and hurried reader to disentangle a text without reading it out loud—Augustine himself was able to do this, as he tells us when describing the tremendous moment of his conversion, when he picks up a volume of Paul's *Epistles* and reads "in silence" the oracular line that tells him to "put on Christ like an armour." But reading out loud was not only considered normal, it was also considered necessary for the full comprehension of a text. Augustine believed that reading needed to be made present; that within the confines of a page the *scripta*, the written words, had to become *verba*, spoken words, in order to spring into being. For Augustine, the reader had literally to breathe life into a text, to fill the created space with living language.

By the ninth century, punctuation and the greater diffusion of books had established silent reading as common, and a new element—privacy—had become a feature of the craft. For these new readers, silent reading allowed a sort of amorous intimacy with the text, creating invisible walls around them and the activity of reading. Seven centuries later, Carpaccio would have considered silent reading part and parcel of the scholar's work, and his scholarly Augustine would necessarily be pictured in a private and quiet place.

Almost five centuries later, in our time, since silent reading is no longer surprising and since we are always desperately searching for novelty, we have managed to grant the text on the screen its own (albeit gratingly disembodied) voice. At the reader's request, a CD-ROM can now usurp the post-Augustine reader's magical prerogative: it can be either silent as a saint while I scan the scrolling page, or lend a text both voice and graphic features, bringing the dead back to life not through a function of memory and a sense of pleasure (as Augustine proposed), but through mechanics, as a ready-made golem whose appearance will no doubt be perfected in time. The difference is, the computer's reading voice isn't our voice: therefore the tone, modulation, emphasis and other instruments for making sense of a text have been established outside our understanding. We have not as much given wing to the *verba* as made the dead *scripta* walk.

Nor is the computer's memory the same as our own. For Augustine, those readers who read the Scriptures in the right spirit preserved the text in the mind, relaying its immortality from reader to reader, throughout the generations. "They read it without interruption," he wrote in the *Confessions*, "and what they read never passes away." Augustine praises these readers who "become" the book itself by carrying the text within them, imprinted in the mind as on a wax tablet.

Being able to remember passages from the essential texts for argument and comparison was still important in Carpaccio's time. But after the invention of printing, and with the increasing custom of private libraries, access to books for immediate consultation became much easier, and sixteenth-century readers were able to rely far more on the books' memory than on their own. The multiple pivoting lectern depicted by Carpaccio in Augustine's study extended the reader's memory even further, as did other wonderful contraptions—such as the marvellous "rotary reading desk" invented in 1588 by the Italian engineer Agostino Ramelli, which allowed a reader ready access to ten different books at almost the same time, each one open at the required chapter and verse.

The capacious memory of my word processor attempts to provide the same service. In certain ways it is vastly superior to those Renaissance inventions. For instance:

The ancient texts of the Greeks and Romans, so rare that many of the books we call classics were unknown to Augustine, were lovingly and laboriously collected by Carpaccio's contemporaries. Today all those texts are entirely at my disposal. Two-thirds of all surviving Greek literature up to the time of Alexander, 3,400,000 words and 24,000 images, can be found contained in four disks published by Yale University Press, so that now, with one nibble from my mouse, I can determine exactly how many times Aristophanes used the word for "man," and figure out that it was twice as often as he used the word for "woman." To come up with such precise statistics, Augustine would have had to strain very hard his mnemonic capacities, even though the art of memory, arduously developed since the days of Greece and Rome, had by then been perfected to an astonishing degree.

However, what my computerized memory cannot do is select and combine, gloss and associate through a mingling of practice and intuition. It can't, for instance, tell me that, in spite of the statistical evidence, it is Aristophanes' women—Praxagora in *The Assemblywomen*, the market gossips in *The Poet and the Women*, that old battle-axe Lysistrata—who come to mind when I think of his work read not on CD but in the ancient Garnier codexes we used at school. The gluttonous memory of my computer is not an active memory, like Augustine's; it is a repository, like Augustine's library, albeit vaster and perhaps more readily accessible. Thanks to my computer, I can memorize—but I can't remember. That is a craft I must learn from Augustine and his ancient codexes.

By Augustine's time, the codex, the book of bound sheets, had supplanted the scroll almost completely, since the codex held, over the scroll, obvious advantages. The scroll allowed for only certain parts of the text to be shown at a given moment, without permitting the reader to flip through pages or read one chapter while keeping another open with a finger. It therefore laid strictures on the reading sequence. The text was offered to the reader in a predetermined order and only one section at a time. A novel like Julio Cortázar's *Hopscotch*, which suggests that the reader choose any sequence of its chapters, would have been unthinkable in the days of the scroll. Also, the scroll limited the contents of the text far more than the codex would ever do. It is surmised that the division of the *Odyssey* into books corresponds not to the poet's desire but to the necessity of what would fit on one scroll.

Today my computer partakes of both book forms: "scrolling" to read a text and yet, if I wish, capable of flipping simultaneously to another section on a separate "window." But in neither case does it have the full characteristics of its elders: it doesn't tell me, as the scroll did at a glance, the full physical measure of its contents. Nor does it allow me, in spite of "windows," to skip and choose pages as dexterously as the codex. On the other hand, my computer is a better retriever: its sniffing-out and fetching functions are infinitely superior to its dog-eared ancestors of parchment and paper.

Augustine knew (and we seldom remember) that every reader creates, when reading, an imaginary space, a space made up of the person reading and the realm of the words read—what Keats called "that purple-lined palace of sweet sin." This reading space exists either in the very medium that reveals or contains it (in the book or in the computer) or in its own textual being, incorporeal, as words preserved in the course of time, a place in the reader's mind. Depending on whether the written word lies at the end or the beginning of a given civilization, whether we see it as the result of a creative process (as did the Greeks) or as the source (as did the Hebrews), the written word becomes—or does not become, as the case may be—the driving force of that civilization.

What I mean is this: for the Greeks, who assiduously wrote down their philosophical treatises, plays, poems, letters, speeches and commercial transactions, and yet regarded the written word merely as a mnemonic aid, the book was an adjunct to civilized life, never its core; for this reason, the material representation of Greek civilization was in space, in the stones of their cities. For the Hebrews, however, whose daily transactions were oral and whose literature was entrusted largely to memory, the book—the Bible, the revealed word of God—became the core of its civilization, surviving in time, not in space, in the migrations of a nomad people. In a commentary on the Bible, Augustine, coming directly from the Hebrew tradition, noted that words tend towards the quality of music, which finds its being in time and does not have any particular geographical location.

My computer apparently belongs not to the book-centred Hebrew tradition of Augustine, but to the bookless Greek tradition that required monuments in stone. Even though the world-wide web simulates on my screen a borderless space, the words I conjure up owe their existence to the familiar temple of the computer, erected with its portico-like screen above the cobbled esplanade of my keyboard. Like marble for the Greeks, these plastic stones speak (in fact, thanks to the audio functions I mentioned, they *literally* speak). And the ritual of access to cyberspace is in certain ways like the rituals of access to a temple or palace, to a symbolic place that requires preparation and learned conventions, decided by invisible and seemingly all-powerful buffs.

Augustine's reading rituals, performed around the space of his desk and within the space of his room, were nevertheless dispensable, or at the very least, kept changing. He could choose to move about with the text he was reading, or go and lie in bed with his codex, or leave the room and read in the garden (as he did when he heard the words that led to his conversion), or in the solitary desert. Augustine's book, as a container of the text, was essentially variable. For the humanist reader of Carpaccio's time, this variability was of the essence, leading to Aldus Manutius's invention of the companionable pocket-book. And throughout the centuries, the book became increasingly portable, multiple, replaceable—able to be read anywhere, in any position, at any time.

My rituals at the computer depend on a complex technology beyond a layperson's knowledge. Even though a Powerbook can allow me to transport my reading to a cliff in the Grand Canyon (as the ads for Macintosh proclaim), the text still owes its existence to the technology that created and maintains it, and still requires my surrendering to the physical "monument" of the machine itself.

That is why, for Augustine, the words on the page—not the perishable scroll or replaceable codex that held them—had physical solidity, a burning, visible presence. For me, the solidity is in the expensive edifice of the computer, not in the fleeting words. When silent, the phantom text, eerily materializing on the screen and vanishing at the drop of a finger, is certainly different from the sturdy, reassuring, even authoritarian black letters meticulously composed on a piece of parchment or stamped on the page. My electronic text is separated from me by a pane of glass, so that I cannot directly kiss the words as Augustine might have done in his devotion, or inhale the perfume of leather and ink as the contemporaries of Carpaccio did in theirs. This accounts for the difference in the vocabulary used by Augustine and myself to describe the act of reading. Augustine spoke of "devouring" or "savouring" a text—a gastronomical imagery derived from a passage in Ezekiel, in which an angel commands the prophet to eat a book, as later occurs in the Revelation of St. John. I instead speak of "surfing" the web, of "scanning" a text. For Augustine, the text had a material quality that required ingestion. For the computer reader, the text exists only as a surface that is skimmed as he "rides the waves" of information from one cyber-area to another.

Does all this mean that our reading craft has declined, lost its most precious qualities, become debased or impoverished? Or has it rather improved, progressed, perfected itself since Augustine's hesitant days? Or are these meaningless questions?

For many years now we have been prophesying the end of the book and the victory of the electronic media, as if books and electronic media were two gallants competing for the same beautiful reader on the same intellectual battlefield. First film, then television, later video games and VCRs have been cast as the book's destroyers, and certain writers—Sven Birkerts, for example, in *The Gutenberg Elegies*—don't hesitate to use apocalyptic language full of calls for salvation and curses against the Antichrist. All readers may be Luddites at heart—but I think this may be pushing our enthusiasms too far. Technology will not retreat, nor, in spite of countless titles predicting the twilight of the printed word, do the numbers of new books printed every year show signs of diminishing.

And yet changes will occur. It is true that before most great changes in technology, the previous technological form experiences a flourish, a last-minute exuberance. After the invention of the printing press, the number of manuscripts produced in Europe increased dramatically, and canvas painting mushroomed immediately after the invention of photography. And it seems more than likely that, even though the number of printed books is higher than ever, certain genres now available mainly as codexes will give way to other formats, better suited for their purpose. Encyclopaedias, for instance, will find more efficient homes on a CD-ROM, once the technology develops an intelligent cross-referencing system and not one that simply throws up, with mechanical nonchalance, every example, however irrelevant. With such a sharpened tool, it will be far easier for a computer to scan an encyclopaedic disk than for the most studious of readers to seek out the twenty-nine volumes of the *Britannica* for all articles mentioning the term *reading*.

But these are obvious transformations. Essentially, nothing precious need be lost. It may be that the qualities we nostalgically wish to retain in books as they appear now, and as the humanist readers imagined them, will reappear under clever guises in the electronic media. We can already scribble on electronic notepads and there are Powerbooks and digital books further reduced to fit in one's hand. The woman in the subway reading her paperback novel and the man next to her listening to the thud-thud bass of his Walkman, the student making notes on the margins of her textbook and the child playing a hand-held Nintendo by her side, may all combine their instruments (as the home computers do now) in a single portable apparatus that will offer all these textual possibilities: displaying text, reciting, allowing for annotations and proposing playful modes of research on one small portable screen or by some other yet-to-be-invented device. The CD-ROM (and whatever else will take its place in the imminent future) is like Wagner's *Gesamtkunstwerk*, a sort of mini-opera, in which all the senses must come into play in order to recreate a text.

So why do we fear the change?

It isn't likely that reading will lose, in the electronic revolution, its aristocratic qualities. In the blurred childhoods of the past, reading appears either as a duty destined to preserve certain notions of authority (as in the scriptoriums of Mesopotamia and of the European Middle Ages) or as a leisure-class activity throughout our various histories, accorded to those with means or usurped by those without them. Most of our societies (by no means all) have assembled around a book and for these the library became an essential symbol of power. Symbolically, the ancient world ends with the destruction of the Library of Alexandria; symbolically, the twentieth century ends with the rebuilding of the library of Sarajevo.

But the notion of true democratic reading is illusory. Carnegie's nineteenth-century libraries were temples to his class where the common readers were allowed to enter, mindful of their position, in veneration of established authority. Reading may bring some measure of social change, as Matthew Arnold believed, but it also can become a way of killing time or of slowing down time against the communality of death, arrogantly set against the monotonous cadence of time spent at work, "doing time" as it were in the countless illiterate sweatshops, mines, fields and factories on which our societies are built.

What will certainly change is the idea of books as property. The notion of the book as an object of value, because of its contents, its history or its decorations, has existed since the days of the scrolls, but it was not until the fourteenth century (in Europe at least) that the rise of a bourgeois audience, beyond the realms of the nobility and the clergy, created a market in which the possession of books became a mark of social standing and the production of books a profit-making business like any other. A whole modern industry arose to fill this commercial need, causing Doris Lessing to exhort her beleaguered fellow workers:

> And it does no harm to repeat, as often as you can, "Without me the literary industry would not exist: the publishers, the agents, the sub-agents, the sub-sub-agents, the accountants, the libel lawyers, the departments of literature, the professors, the theses, the books of criticism, the reviewers, the book pages—all this vast and proliferating

edifice is because of this small, patronized, put-down and underpaid person."

But in the days of the new technology, the industry (which will not disappear) will have to work otherwise in order to survive. Essays on the Internet, poems transmitted through modem, books copied onto disk and passed on from friend to friend have begun to bypass publishers and booksellers. Interactive novels question the very notion of authorship. Who will be paid royalties for a text scanned in Salamanca, received on e-mail in Recife, modified in Melbourne, expanded in Ecuador, saved on a soft disk in San Francisco? Who in fact is the author of that multifarious text? Like the many contributors to the construction of a medieval cathedral or to the production of a Hollywood film, the new industry will find, no doubt, ways of securing a profit for someone, Church or Multinational. And Doris Lessing's small and underpaid person may have to resign herself to becoming even smaller and more underpaid.

This bleak prospect is not, however, without a few stimulating vistas. In January of 1996, shortly after the death of President Mitterrand, the French government, following the age-honoured custom of governments everywhere, banned a book, *Le Grand Secret*. In this book, the president's doctors, Claude Gubier and Michel Gonod, revealed intimate details of their illustrious patient's decline and made public the official efforts to conceal the gravity of his illness. Banning books has always been an assumed prerogative of those in power, and until now writers have had no recourse against edicts and bonfires except samizdat editions and faith in a more tolerant future. Brave words have been spoken from home fires burning or from the waiting-rooms of exile, but the banning of books continues. Until now. On 23 January 1996, Pascal Barbaud, owner of a cybercafé in Besançon where customers can, for a fee, use the café's Internet service, decided to scan *Le Grand Secret* onto the Internet. The Internet was, apparently, beyond any one government's jurisdiction (I say "was" because the censors, with the ancient excuse of the threat of pornography or hate literature, are entering this sanctum too). And so Barbaud succeeded in his subversive mission. Since no one person need be responsible for an Internet text, *Le Grand Secret* became the first banned book openly to escape the powers of the censor.

And yet no reader is ever satisfied. The Internet *Grand Secret* is a mere copying of the printed text. But what if it were opened up to the participation of each Internet user, like the on-screen novels of Robert Coover, to which any reader may add his or her inspiration, or change the beginning or the end? Privileged with the time to read, somewhat freed from the constraints of censorship, in the luxury of a private space, our fearful reader wonders: will we still be able to read critically such an electronic text, a text liable to be transformed by its readers on the screen, a protean (or, in our ugly vocabulary, "interactive") text?

In our fear, we forget that every text is, in a very essential sense, "interactive," changing according to a particular reader at a particular hour and in a particular place. Every single reading carries the reader into the "spiral of interpretation," as the French historian Jean-Marie Pailler has called it. No reading can avoid it, every reading adds a turn to its vertiginous ascent. There never was "pure reading": in reading Diderot, the act becomes confused with conversation; in Danielle Steele with titillation; in Defoe with reportage; in others with instruction, with gossip, with lexicography, with cataloguing, with hysterics. There seems to be no Platonic archetype of any one reading, as there seems to be no Platonic archetype of any one book. The notion of a text being "passive" is only true in the abstract: from the earliest scrolls to the displays of Bauhaus typography, every recorded text, every book in whatever shape, carries implicitly or explicitly an aesthetic intention. No two manuscripts were ever the same, as the arduous cataloguers of Alexandria remarked, forcing them to choose "definitive" versions of the books they were preserving, and establishing in the process the epistemological rule of reading: that every new copy supersedes the previous one, since it must of necessity include it. And while Gutenberg's printing press, recreating the miracle of the loaves and fishes, multiplied one same text a thousand times, every reader proceeds to individualize his or her copy with scribbles, stains, markings of different sorts, so that no copy, once read, is identical to another. All these myriad variations, all these various runs of thumb-printed copies, have not prevented us, however, from speaking of "my very own copy" of *Hamlet* or *King Lear* much as we speak of "the one and only" Shakespeare. Electronic texts will find new ways to generalize and define, and new critics will find vocabularies generous enough to accommodate the possibility of change.

The misplaced fear of technology, which once opposed the codex to the scroll, now opposes the scroll to the codex. It opposes the unfurling text on the screen to the multiple pages of the humanist reader's hand-held book. But all technology, whether satanic mills or satanic Chernobyls, has a human measure; it is impossible to remove the human strand even from the most inhuman of technological devices. They are our creation, even if we try to deny them (as the Red Queen would say) with both hands. Recognizing that human measure, like understanding the exact meaning of the coloured palm marks on the walls of prehistoric caves, may be beyond our present capabilities. What we require therefore is not a new humanist reader but a more effective one, one who will restore to the text now enmeshed in technological devices the ambiguity that lent it a divinatory capacity. What we need is not to marvel at the effects of virtual reality, but to recognize its very real and useful defects, the necessary cracks through which we can enter a space yet uncreated. We need to be less, not more, assertive. Whether, for the future humanist reader, the book in its present form will remain unchanged or not is in some ways an idle question. My guess (but it is no more than a guess) is that by and large it will not change very drastically, because it has adapted so well to our requirements—though these, indeed, may change....

The question I ask myself instead is this: in these new technological spaces, with these artefacts that will certainly coexist with (and in some cases supplant) the book—how will we succeed in still able being to invent, to remember, to learn, to record, to reject, to wonder, to exult, to subvert, to rejoice? By what means will we continue to be creative readers instead of passive viewers?

Almost ten years ago, George Steiner suggested that the anti-bookish movement will drive reading back to its birthplace and that there will be reading-houses like the old monastic libraries, where those of us quaint enough to wish to peruse an old-fashioned book will go and sit and read in silence. Something of the sort is taking place in the Monastery of the Holy Cross in Chicago's South Side, but not in the way Steiner imagined: here the monks, after morning prayers, switch on their IBM computers and work away in their scriptorium like their ancestors a thousand years ago, copying and glossing and preserving texts for future generations. And even the privacy of devotional reading will not, apparently, retreat into secrecy; it has instead become ecumenical: God Himself can apparently be reached via the Jerusalem "Wailing Wall" Internet site for readers of the Old Testament, or via the Vatican's Pope-site for readers of the New.

To these visions of future reading, I would like to add three more, imagined not too long ago by Ray Bradbury.

- In one of the stories of *The Martian Chronicles*, "There Will Come Soft Rains," a fully automatized house offers, as an evening diversion, to read a poem to its inhabitants, and when it receives no response it selects and reads a poem on its own, unaware that the entire family has been annihilated in a nuclear war. This is the future of reading without readers.
- Another story, "Usher II," records the saga of a heroic devotee of Poe in an age when fiction is considered not a source for thought but something dangerously real. After Poe's works are outlawed, this passionate reader builds a weird and dangerous house as a shrine to his hero, through which he destroys both his enemies and the books he intends to avenge. This is the future of readers without reading.
- The third, the most famous, is in *Fahrenheit 451*, and depicts a future in which books are burned and groups of literature lovers have memorized their favourite books, carrying them around in their heads like walking libraries. This is a future in which readers and reading, in order to survive, follow Augustine's precept and become one and the same.

Automated reading that requires no readers; the act of reading left to old-fashioned cranks who believe in books not as monsters but as places for dialogue; books transformed into a memory carried about until the mind caves in and the spirit fails ... These scenarios suit the last years of our century: the end of books set against the end of time, the end of the second millennium. At the end of the first, the Adamites burnt their libraries before joining their brethren in preparation for the Apocalypse, so as not to carry useless wisdom into the promised Kingdom of Heaven.

Our fears are endemic fears, rooted in our time. They don't branch into the unknowable future, they demand a conclusive answer, here and now. "Stupidity," wrote Flaubert, "consists in a desire to conclude."

Indeed. As every reader knows, the point, the essential quality of the act of reading, now and always, is that it tends to no foreseeable end, to no conclusion. Every reading prolongs another, begun in some afternoon thousands of years ago and of which we know nothing; every reading projects its shadow onto the following page, lending it content and context. In this way, the story grows, layer after layer, like the skin of the society whose history the act preserves. In Carpaccio's painting, Augustine sits, as attentive as his dog, pen poised, book shining like a screen, looking straight into the light, listening. The room, the instruments keep changing, the books on the shelf shed their covers, the texts tell stories in voices not yet born.

The waiting continues.

ABOUT THE TYPE

This book was set in *Bulmer*, a typeface originally cut by William Martin in about 1790 for William Bulmer of the Shakespeare Press. Martin's types are reminiscent of Baskerville's and were promoted by the printer, whose name became attached to them.